Seeing the Whole Elephant:

An Essential Guide to Viewing Reality from God's Perspective

How can we see reality from God's perspective?

A Quick User's Guide to
Seeing the Whole Elephant

Grasp the importance of seeing with a biblical worldview.	Part One
Avoid common distortions about God, and then love Him with our whole heart, mind, and soul.	Part Two
See people as God does so we can better obey the second Greatest Commandment.	Part Three
Clearly see our assignment, the Great Commission, from the perspective of each of the Gospels and Acts.	Part Four
Learn practical strategies for sharper spiritual perception! There is no single, silver bullet for seeing clearly, but these strategies will greatly improve our spiritual sight!	Part Five

Endorsements

In *Seeing the Whole Elephant*, Nick offers to clean the lenses of the reader's perception by addressing contemporary issues using historical contexts. By clearly explaining the connection between the past and present, he shines a light in the dark and brings focus out of obscurity. His accounts of historical and current believers dispel present-day myths, misunderstandings, and misnomers about the beauty of following Christ wholeheartedly. Nick's academic and practical insights will help you better see reality from God's perspective.

—**Greg Mundis**
Executive Director
Assemblies of God World Missions

I once walked out of a Russian Banya with the feeling that something was terribly wrong. I was dizzy and confused. My vision was blurred and out of focus. My walk was erratic and unsteady. Was I having a stroke or some other terrible physical calamity? Then I realized that the intense heat of the Banya had affected the surface of my plastic progressive lenses. A new set of lenses set everything right. I have known Nick Robertson for many years and have come to appreciate his clear thinking and laser focus on reaching the world's least reached people with the gospel message. *Seeing the Whole Elephant* is an effective tool to help all of us see more clearly.

—**Omar J. Beiler**
Eurasia Regional Director
Assemblies of God World Missions

Our eyes spotlight not only what we see physically, but also how we interpret life and its meaning. *Seeing the Whole Elephant* will help you add a spiritual lens to what you are seeing in culture, the Church, and throughout the world. Nick has done a masterful job of weaving together life stories, world culture, and a strong apologetic to help us clearly see God, ourselves, and others. I know this book will transform the way you see and live.

—**Jeff Hartensveld**
Asia Pacific Regional Director
Assemblies of God World Missions

In *Seeing the Whole Elephant,* Nick Robertson has produced a work that helps the reader see as God sees—how God sees us, the world, and the lost. Nick helps us to realize that all worldviews are not correct. Only a worldview that is biblically based and sees the world with God's eyes can provide a right perspective on the lost. In this book, filled with practical examples and real-life stories, Nick challenges us to not only see clearly, but to become proactive about what we see—to fulfill the Great Commission. I recommend this book to every pastor, missionary, student, and individual believer—so that all may see more clearly.

—**Ron Maddux**
Former Northern Asia Regional Director
Assemblies of God World Missions

Seeing the Whole Elephant is exactly right. Nick Robertson sheds a powerful light on the problem of the unreached world. He articulates it thoughtfully and gives beautiful insight. But then he adds something far more to the conversation, namely, practical solutions. This is easy to read and practical, yet deeply insightful at the same time. A fantastic read!!!

—**Neal Rich**
Lead Pastor
Cedar Valley Church, Bloomington, MN

When Jesus sees the world, He sees that there are over 3.15 billion people in 7,000 unreached people groups making up 42 percent of our world. An Unreached People is a gathering of those with their own language, culture, and religion, but without Christians—or with so few that there are not enough local disciples, Bibles, and churches for the gospel to advance without missionary presence and partnership. Nick helps us see this clearly, and then helps us see what we should do about it. It's a priceless vision.

—**Dick Brogden**
Co-Founder
Live Dead Movement

In *Seeing the Whole Elephant*, Nick Robertson reminds us that the development of our worldview is not a once-and-for-all exercise where we 'get it right' for all time. It is forged in a relationship with the living God that then shapes our relationship with others and is nurtured in spiritual disciplines in the course of everyday life. This book is a much needed voice to help imprint on our hearts that truly meeting the living God sets us on a path to seeing the world the way He sees it and being caught up in His redemptive mission to those who lack access to the good news of what God has done in Jesus Christ.

—**Alan Johnson**
Missionary to Thailand
Assemblies of God World Missions

Nick Robertson is a top tier leader with a proven missional heart. If anyone could be an influence in the area of seeing with the eyes of the Spirit, Nick can. His personal ministry is living proof of what he has written. I would highly recommend *Seeing the Whole Elephant* to anyone who is looking for insight into their own personal spiritual journey.

—**Frank Potter**
Superintendent
Potomac Network of the Assemblies of God

I first met Nick in India, and from the beginning, his passion to make Christ known was compelling. His writing will challenge you to see a lost world through God's eyes. The strategies he presents are practical and build on solid scriptural principles. Your vision of the future will be altered as you consider God's perspective presented through the pages of this book.

—**Mark Dean**
Superintendent
Minnesota District Council of the Assemblies of God

I must confess that until I read Nick's book, I was unaware the Bible had so much to say about how we see things. This book brings fresh revelation to the whole idea of how we see God, how we see ourselves, how we see others, and many other insights concerning the power of biblical and spiritual sight. Nick's many illustrations and stories make the biblical text come alive. This is a must-read as far as I am concerned.

—**Don James**
Superintendent
New Jersey Ministry Network of the Assemblies of God

Through his excellent book, *Seeing the Whole Elephant*, Nick Robertson captures how the worldview of many is skewed with a blurred vision of true reality by our present culture and by the enemy of our soul. Using the Word of God, he helps believers see how their worldview can be shifted and corrected to align with God's view. By following the prescriptions of the author, believers will not only have clearer spiritual vision but will also develop a deeper hunger for intimacy with God. After reading this book, you will be challenged and motivated to seek Him will all your heart. May this book ignite a fire within believers to live counter-culturally and radically impact their world for Christ!

—Don Miller
Superintendent
Southern Missouri District of the Assemblies of God

Developing a clear, godly worldview is important for every Christian. How we view God, ourselves, and others is critical to how we approach life. This book leads the reader to consider all of these, providing particular insight into Jesus' Great Commission and putting forth strategies to develop clearer vision in the midst of our present worldly challenges. This practical book will make you think, sort, and apply—always a fulfilling process.

—Carolyn Tennant
Author; Professor Emerita at North Central University, Minneapolis;
and faculty in the D.Min. program at the Assemblies of God Theological
Seminary of Evangel University, Springfield, MO

Today's generation of university students is fatigued by what they consider fake and plastic as well as the ambiguity they have endured in our present culture. Despite the relativism we hear about, I have discovered this generation is in pursuit of answers and truth. Nick embarks on a journey with the reader, unveiling and adeptly answering the pragmatic and relevant questions being considered by today's students. *Seeing The Whole Elephant* is engaging, timely, and adroitly apologetic. Nick's writing is a gift to university students; both the inquirer and the Christian committed to "always being prepared to make a defense to anyone who asks you for a reason for the hope that is in you" (1 Peter 3: 15 ESV).

—**Scott Martin**
National Director
Chi Alpha Campus Ministries, USA

With a generation hungrier than ever for spiritual fathers, Nick's timely and accessible writing addresses a significant felt need among young believers. Decades of personal investment in helping others discover their destiny comes through in every page of *Seeing the Whole Elephant*. Read this book if you want to be inspired, encouraged, and challenged to live with clear eyes and purpose to discover your role in God's global plan!

—**Nathan Cole**
Operations Director
Chi Alpha Campus Ministries, USA

Imagine yourself moving tentatively through a vast, inky-dark basement. You make a mental map to understand where you have been and where you hope to go. Your map includes your best guesses about the objects you have already run into, places that felt safe, and the things your toes kicked in the dark. Then, an unseen person strikes a match! As unfamiliar, wonderful light fills the air, you are shocked to see terrifying holes in the floor, some quite near, including one just ahead in the direction you were planning to go. You also see objects of unexpected value, a surprising number of fellow searchers scattered all over the room, and one thing more—a sturdy stairway, leading up into the daylight. When Nick Robertson wrote *Seeing the Whole Elephant*, he lit a match bright enough to help you see your own life and world in God's surprising light.

Nick's lifetime of intercultural ministry experience will help you stop, think, and act with God in mind. This book is a practical theology of God's view of reality as expressed in the Bible. Nick can help you see your life, your world, and your purpose clearly. He will also give you a handful of priceless matches you can use to help other searchers who have never seen a light bright enough to reveal their world at all. Read it; then study it with a person you want to disciple, re-read it with your spouse, or give it to a friend!

—**Paul York**
Cross Cultural Missions Training
Chi Alpha Campus Ministries, USA

Seeing the Whole Elephant:

An Essential Guide to Viewing Reality from God's Perspective

Nick Robertson

Foreword by Scott Hagan

Seeing the Whole Elephant:
An Essential Guide to Viewing Reality
from God's Perspective

Manufactured in the U.S.A. 2021

Cover design and interior layout design by Uberwriters Christian Ghostwriters
www.uberwriters.com

ISBN 978-1-7379920-0-4 Paperback
ISBN 978-1-7379920-1-1 eBook

THE
ANTIOCH
INITIATIVE

Dedication

This book is dedicated to my parents who have blessed me and my family in innumerable ways.

(1) Both lived as authentic Christians, loving God and seeing both the reality of the spirit world and the reality of eternity.

(2) Both loved me and communicated their love for me consistently. I have been extremely blessed to never question the reality of their love for me. Their love for me has further helped me better understand and live in God's love.

(3) Both my parents enjoyed life and used their resources to make a difference in the lives of others. As lay people they were very involved in ministry through their local church. They also went on thirteen short-term overseas missions trips, using dentistry as a tool for the Kingdom. God used my parents' hearts for the nations to impact me and His calling on my life. I am very grateful for their example.

Table of Contents

Foreword

*"Leaders are able to see things that the rest
of the world is only looking at."*
—Scott Hagan

Our society is reeling. Foundations have dissolved. Clarity feels
fluid and elusive. Even Christian doctrine, previously accepted by
most in the church as eternal, is being repackaged with remarkable
speed as nothing more than experiments of context. Much like the
incarcerated Apostle Paul *en route* to Rome, our whole world is
trapped and adrift in a violent storm. But instead of despair and
retreat, hidden 'captains' are emerging from the bowels of the ship
with a fresh word from the Lord. Though in chains, and without
the reassurance of daylight for fourteen days, Paul's intimacy with
Christ never wavered, even as the ship began to break apart. Down
in the darkest compartments of the ship, the Lord was honoring
Paul's faith and passion with clarity for every passenger on board.
I see the same phenomenon happening today.

Dr. Nick Robertson's helpful new work, *Seeing the Whole
Elephant*, blends doctrine with demonstration. Beginning with the
reaffirmation of a biblical worldview, Nick Robertson clears away
the fog of false teaching and directs the reader toward a more
prolific prophetic life missionally rooted in the Great Commission.
Seeing the Whole Elephant was born out of Nick's burden to see
revival and the Great Commission activated at the personal level;
it will inspire Christians everywhere to access the full prophetic
arsenal provided them.

Whether you are spiritually minded or divided by secular
arguments, the gifts of the Spirit are a divine intrusion into the

routines and traditions of modern and post-modern life. In a day and age where 'cultural fit' dominates our list of core values, *Seeing the Whole Elephant* is a powerful handbook.

The predicament for many believers and pastors involves examining the chemistry between their own authentic encounters with the Holy Spirit and the experiences and expressions of others that may feel far less authentic and doctrinal than their own. This anxiety has caused some to discard their prophetic role—divorcing themselves from the preciousness of prophecy and the gifts of the Spirit. As messy as people's operation in the gifts can be, the gifts of the Spirit were never intended to be a distraction or burden to the church. Not only is the person of the Holy Spirit a gift, but He also came to distribute even more gifts to and through the Church.

The evil of neighbor devouring neighbor is rooted in the false teaching of our day. This demands that we see clearly. We must view ourselves, and the nations we are called to reach, with greater biblical accuracy. We cannot be instruments of narcissism; we must be instruments of service. *Seeing the Whole Elephant* gives you the practical steps for culturing a Spirit-spilled life. The Holy Spirit right now is opening the gates of hostile nations, it's time we enter those gates in the same fullness of the Spirit's power.

—**Scott Hagan, Ph.D.**
President, North Central University
Minneapolis, MN

Preface

Years ago, I wrote *Hearing God's Voice Today*, which looks at how we hear God in our everyday life. After writing that book, I soon began to grasp that just as the ear is important for hearing God, our spiritual eyes are critical for grasping what He is doing in our world.

Perhaps no other physical sense is valued more than our sense of sight. Being able to see clearly spiritually is necessary to walking with the Holy Spirit through life. How we perceive God, others, and what is going on around us, greatly impacts our actions.

Our family was blessed to live in Asia for many years and noted significant differences in how people from various cultures, religions, economic backgrounds, and worldviews see the world. How we perceive reality greatly impacts our thoughts, which greatly impact how we see and make decisions.

As our family has shifted back to the United States for a season, we have noted both the strong influence of secularism on American culture and a shift away from considering eternity as real.

Though Western culture has changed, God has not, and neither have the realities of eternity and the spiritual nature of life. More than ever, we need God's help to see the whole elephant, to see reality from God's perspective.

This book is a tool to help Christ followers see more clearly. The spirit world and eternity are real. Though our human sight is limited, God can see the whole picture, the whole elephant.

Acknowledgments

Many have contributed to the finalization of this work. I am grateful for many friends and colleagues who have given of their expertise and wisdom to this book.

First of all, gratitude and thanks go to my family who have endured with me as I have worked on this book for many months. My wife, in particular, has edited most of this work and has been a consistent encouragement. She consistently helps me improve my written expression and gave excellent suggestions for the title and structure of the book. She further assisted greatly with the questions at the end of each chapter. My girls, too, have been quite patient through multiple revisions and conversations about this book's contents.

Further, I want to give thanks to many friends who have critiqued and given valuable feedback on the content of this book.

Allen Tennison gave multiple insights into chapters 2 and 3, particularly with regard to representing secularists more clearly.

Dick Brogden gave valuable correction and insights into chapter 4 regarding the Great Commission.

Glen Davis gave excellent feedback on the text as a whole and perspective for content for Chi Alpha students.

Nathan Cole gave multiple suggestions and had multiple recommendations for connecting with Chi Alpha Nation!

Paul York shared some of his vast multicultural insights and gave excellent feedback on connecting with students, especially in Chi Alpha.

Alan Johnson's insights regarding Buddhism are much appreciated and helped me portray Buddhist thought more accurately.

Carolyn Tennant's feedback and guidance with publishing recommendations were a great blessing.

Ben Wagner and Sam Keefe have encouraged and prayed with me many times during the writing of this book and have offered valuable feedback.

Lois Olena's editing assistance was also invaluable and insightful.

Finally, I am very grateful to Scott Hagan for encouragement and feedback and his writing of the foreword for *Seeing the Whole Elephant*.

Introduction

In an Indian folktale, six blind men try to identify an unknown animal, which the audience is told is an elephant. Each man reaches out to touch the animal and then describes to the others what he feels with his fingers. What the men do not realize is that each of them is unknowingly touching a different part of the animal. The first approaches the elephant's side and proclaims the animal to be like a wall. The second approaches the elephant's tusk and declares the animal is like a spear. Grabbing the animal's trunk, the third man pronounces the creature to be like a snake. The fourth approaches the animal's knee and proclaims the elephant is like a tree. Feeling the animal's ear, the fifth man compares the animal with a fan. Finally, the sixth man grabs the animal's tail and likens the elephant to a rope.

John Godfrey Saxe popularized this tale through his poem "The Blind Men and the Elephant."[1] In his poem Saxe describes the blind men as being limited by their "seeing" only *parts* of the elephant. The blind men misidentified the animal because no man "saw" the whole animal, but rather just the part he touched.

Many people have referenced Saxe's poem to discredit Christianity and other worldviews that make truth claims. However, this use of the poem backfires because this usage implies that those who make truth claims are wrong or even arrogant. Yet, the author commits the same error by making the truth claim that he can see not just part, but *all* the elephant. The narrator assumes the superior place of having a better view of reality than all the others in the story. He claims the very knowledge the others do not have.

The truth is only God can see the whole elephant; only God can see all of reality. As humans we are extremely limited in our perceptual ability, but there is hope. We can grow in our ability to see. God, who can see all, wants to help us see as He does. *Seeing the Whole Elephant* is a guide to help us see from God's perspective.

The first part of the book addresses our need for God's help in seeing clearly, the role of faith in everyone's worldview, and our need to see the world with a biblical worldview. Just as the blind men struggled to identify the elephant, we struggle today when we try to grasp reality without God's assistance. Contrary to the popular saying, "All roads lead to the top of the mountain," not all worldviews lead to the same destination. We need God's perspective to make sure we are on the right road!

The second and third parts of this book examine the two most important parts of our worldview—how we view God and how we view people. These two parts relate with the two Old Testament commands Christ recognized as the greatest: to love God with our whole heart, mind, and strength, and to love our neighbor as ourselves (Matt 22:37-39).[2] Having a clear view of God and the value of people enables us to see much more clearly in life.

The fourth part of this book examines the Great Commission, our assignment as Christians while on earth. Each gospel writer uniquely articulates the Great Commission and insights can be gleaned from each version. Believers must see their assignment well and grow in understanding their individual roles.

The fifth part of the book looks at practical steps we can take to see better. It is not enough to simply want to see better; we must take steps to improve our spiritual acuity. Practices like humility, thankfulness, obedience and focusing on God's greatness can help us see better spiritually. Each of the fifteen keys found in this section provide insights into enhancing our spiritual perception: prayer, focusing on the Bible, looking beyond the natural world, being humble and thankful, connecting with Christ's Body, seeking the baptism of the Holy Spirit, growing in spiritual gifts, keeping a sabbath, avoiding the distractions of sin and lies, obeying what we already see, renewing our minds, and focusing on God's greatness. By following these strategies, we can grow in our ability to spiritually see our circumstances and the world from God's perspective.

Jesus said, "The eye is the lamp of the body. So, if your eye is healthy, your whole body will be full of light, but if your eye is bad, your whole body will be full of darkness! (Matt 6:22-23).[3] My prayer is that God will grant you, the reader of this book, increased clarity of vision as you navigate life. May you see reality from God's perspective.

PART ONE:

Seeing with a Biblical Worldview

"Your word is a lamp to my feet
and a light to my path."
Psalm 119:105

CHAPTER ONE

HELP NEEDED!

"Do you see a man who is wise in his own eyes?
There is more hope for a fool than for him."
Proverbs 26:12

In "The Blind Men and the Elephant," both the blind men and the storyteller are limited in their ability to see. The storyteller may see better than the men who were physically blind, but his sight was also restricted. He saw enough of the animal to identify it as an elephant, but he could not see the entire elephant at once. If looking at the elephant's left side, he could not at that moment also see the elephant's right side. While looking into the elephant's eyes, he would not be able to see its tail. Neither could he see inside the elephant at its internal anatomy, nor inside the thinking of the animal.

All humans are limited in visual acuity. All humans have inherent visual limitations. Even if we have perfect 20/20 vision, it is still four to five times less than an eagle's vision. Even if we have excellent peripheral vision, our vision pales in comparison to that of a horse, which can see about 350 degrees, almost fully behind itself. Humans need microscopes to see germs and telescopes to see most stars and galaxies. As we age, we often need glasses with increasing strength to read and navigate life.

Time also limits our perception. We only live seventy, eighty, ninety, maybe one hundred years. Our time living on earth is short compared to the many years combined humans have lived before us. So much has preceded us in history. While we can see some periphery—some into the past and a bit into the future—our clearest perceptions are limited to the here and now. Furthermore, what and how we see is also impacted by which time period we live in and what the media allows us to see.

Geography limits our vision even more. Though travel is amazing in our age, we can still only be in one place at a time. Life is happening on seven different continents on earth in about 200 different countries. There is no way we can have a comprehensive view of what is happening everywhere. The vast majority of life happens where we are not! We might as well get over FOMO (fear of missing out)—it is inevitable!

We learn much from the writings of humans who have lived before us, but their perspectives were also limited. Those before us had even less access to tools we have now for seeing well. Most of what has happened on earth was never even recorded.

Additionally, all written history is colored by what a particular author or person chose to see of 'the elephant.' History is written by the "winners," but the winners do not see everything. Today much history is being rewritten because people want to see themselves and their people in more positive ways and because important contributions have been overlooked.

Our processing capacity further limits our perception. We do not all have genius IQs, and that's okay. Let's imagine, however, that every person on planet Earth was a genius, and we harnessed everyone's mental capacities—there would still be a limit to what humans can understand, process, and remember. The Apostle Paul confirmed our human limitations when writing, "Now we see things imperfectly, like puzzling reflections in a mirror, but then we will see everything with perfect clarity" (1 Cor 13:12 NLV). Paul's words remind us that we all need help with seeing.

It often turns out that we experience the same difficulty the blind men faced. We only see one part of an event in our lives, one section of life, one segment of an issue. This faulty vision can cause us to draw some wrong conclusions, make some poor decisions, and live with misconceptions and lies.

Even though we can never hope to see everything, we can get better at our perception. How is that possible? Because we have the opportunity of knowing someone who can see the 'whole elephant'—God!

Here's some good news: God wants to help us see better!

God sees the entire universe. Nothing escapes His view. He sees the big picture and sees each one of us—our pasts, our presents, and our futures. He sees our natures and purposes. He designed us and sees everything about us!

Here's some good news: God wants to help us see better! He wants to help us understand who He is and who we are. He wants to help us fulfill the purpose for which He created us. He wants to give us a clear vision for our lives. He also wants us to have a biblical worldview so we can better interpret what we see in life.

How Do You See It?

1. In what ways is your human perception limited?

2. Think back to a wrong conclusion you have drawn or a bad decision you have made—what faulty perspective led you down this path?

3. The Apostle Paul wrote, "Now we see things imperfectly, like puzzling reflections in a mirror, but then we will see everything with perfect clarity" (1 Cor 13:12 NLV). How do you think our perception will be different in heaven?

CHAPTER TWO

SEEING THROUGH A DIFFERENT LENS

"Everyone has a worldview whether they realize it or not. It is not only a human prerogative, but a human necessity."[1]

The rainy season that year had been the heaviest ever, and the rivers had broken their banks. There were floods everywhere, and the animals were all running up into the hills; the water came so fast that many of the animals drowned. Birds, of course, were able to fly to safety. Some of the leopards climbed to safety, as long as the trees they were able to climb withstood the onslaught of the water. Monkeys, with their proverbial agility to climb up into the treetops and swing from branch to branch, were largely safe.

As the monkeys looked down on the surface of the water, they saw fish swimming and gracefully jumping through the water. One of the monkeys, seeing the fish, shouted to his companions: "Look down, my friends, look at those poor creatures. They are going to drown. Do you see how they struggle in the water?"

"Yes," cried the other monkeys. "What a pity! Probably they were late in escaping to the hills because they seem to have no legs. How can we save them?"

Another monkey said, "I think we must do something. Let's go close to the edge of the flood where the water is not deep enough to cover us, and we can help them to get out."

The monkeys did just that. They started catching the fish, but not without difficulty. One by one, they brought them out of the water and put them carefully on the dry land. After a short time, there was a pile of fish lying on the grass motionless.

One of the monkeys said, "Do you see? They were tired, but now they are just sleeping and resting. Had it not been for us, all these poor creatures without legs would have drowned."

Another monkey replied, "They were trying to escape from us because they could not understand our good intentions. But when they wake up, they will be very grateful."[2]

The monkeys clearly misread the situation entirely. When the fish were thriving, the monkeys saw them as dying. When the fish were actually dying, the monkeys saw them as sleeping. Now, of course, this story is fictitious, but it well illustrates the limitations of one's worldview. James Sire defines worldview as,

> ... a commitment, a fundamental orientation of the heart, that can be expressed as a story or in a set of presuppositions (assumptions which may be true, partially true or entirely false) that we hold (consciously or subconsciously, consistently or inconsistently) about the basic constitution of reality, and that

provides the foundation on which we live and move and have our being.[3]

People do not always realize the scope and impact of their own worldview. This often leads them to inconsistencies in their beliefs and behaviors. One's presuppositions impact behavior, whether those presuppositions are fully understood or not.

How we see the world has profound implications for ourselves, the people around us, and creation itself. How we view circumstances, events, actions, and people impacts our behavior and priorities. This is true, regardless of whether the orientations of our hearts and minds are conscious or subconscious.

In our story, the monkeys' worldview was totally different from that of the fish. The monkeys could not comprehend another creature living in water and not drowning. As land animals, they could only understand living beings surviving on land. The monkeys' worldview assumption—no animal can survive under-water—led the monkeys to kill the fish.

Just as the monkeys' worldview controlled how they saw the world, so too our worldviews control how we see the world. Researchers of culture often equate our worldview to "glasses" we wear over our eyes. Everyone wears such a "pair of glasses," even if he or she is unaware of it. Every person has a worldview, and the lenses of our worldview affect what and how we see.

Worldviews answer life's biggest questions: How did the world begin? What is my purpose in life? What are the problems in life, and how can they be remedied? Are there morals? If so, how are morals determined? As humans, we are wired to want to know the answers to these questions. We want to know where the world came from and why we are here on the planet. We want to know why bad things happen and how we can avoid them. We want to feel good about ourselves, and we desperately search for ways to make ourselves feel better about this life we are living. The worldview we choose gives us answers to these life questions

9

and provides us with a framework to evaluate what is happening around us.

Worldviews are part of being human. James Anderson humorously compares worldviews to belly buttons: everyone has one, but we do not discuss them very often. Anderson gives an even better analogy of worldviews being like cerebellums: everyone has one and needs one, but not everyone knows they have one.[4]

No one's view of life is truly "neutral" because everyone has worldview commitments. Some people are aware of these commitments, but many people are not. Often people do not think through the implications of what they say they believe. People's worldviews can also be inconsistent. They may live one way while saying they believe something else. What reveals our true worldview, however, is what we show it to be by our words and actions. Our worldview affects the way we view life and therefore the way we make decisions, prioritize, behave, and do life.

No one's view of life is truly "neutral" because everyone has worldview commitments. Some people are aware of these commitments, but many people are not.

Some of the broad categories of worldviews include a theistic worldview (any worldview that believes in God), naturalism (a worldview that excludes God and anything incapable of being understood scientifically), Buddhism, Islam, and pantheistic worldviews such as Hinduism. Within any category, many variations exist. Regardless of how a person chooses to label his or her worldview, everyone has one, and that worldview will affect every area of life.

One day when I was doing some work around the house, I inadvertently picked up a pair of my wife's reading glasses and put them on. Her glasses were the same color and shape as mine, but a different (weaker) prescription. I became frustrated because, even with squinting, I struggled to make out the letters I was reading. The glasses were *not* working, and why was my head starting to hurt? Having the right prescription matters!

If our worldview "glasses" have the wrong prescription, our vision gets distorted. Our perception of reality is warped. Truth can look false, and false can look true. We need God's help in wearing the right pair of "glasses!"

The authors of *Making Sense of Your World* suggest four tests for evaluating whether or not a worldview is true:

1. Test of reason: Is it reasonable? Can it be logically stated and defended?

2. Test of the outer world: Is there some external, corroborating evidence to support it?

3. Test of the inner world: Does it adequately address the victories, disappointments, blessings, crises, and relationships in our everyday world?

4. Test of the real world: Are its consequences good or bad when applied in any given cultural context?[5]

These tests serve as guidelines for examining whether a worldview is worth following. Seeing the world differently leads to different understandings of what is important and what truly leads to human flourishing. Different understandings of reality lead to vastly different actions.

The monkeys unwittingly caused great damage to the fish. Their skewed worldview caused chaos and death. In the same way, when we have a faulty worldview or skewed view of reality, we end up tolerating, condoning, and possibly promoting ideas and actions that are against the heart of God and harmful to humanity. Worldviews have consequences, not only for us but for the people and world around us.

How Do You See It?

1. What types of worldviews do you regularly encounter?

2. What is an example of how co-workers or friends' worldviews led them to a totally different conclusion than yours?

3. We often do not think through the implications of what we say we believe. Can you give an example from your own life?

CHAPTER THREE

DO YOU HAVE THE RIGHT PRESCRIPTION?

"All roads lead to the judgment seat of Christ."[1]
—*Keith Green*

We live in a world in which people hold radically different worldviews, and yet, a common narrative persists that all these views are basically the same. We are told that it does not really matter whether someone is a Hindu, agnostic, or Muslim—all paths are valid and lead to a similar or at least favorable destination. Really? By this logic, the next time I want to fly to Atlanta, I should be able to go to the airport, enter any plane I choose, and expect to land in Atlanta. Similarly, some say, "All paths lead to the top of the mountain." Really? Some paths circle the mountain. Some lead to other mountains. Other paths lead down the mountain.

All paths do not lead to the top of a mountain, and all worldviews are not the same. Going back to the analogy of the eyeglasses, each worldview has a distinct prescription for its lenses. The prescription in our particular eyeglasses affects what we see. Radically different interpretations of reality result from different prescriptions, as illustrated by the following story:

> Three friends went to a nature preserve in the African Serengeti and experienced the majestic beauty and diversity of African wildlife. They were able to view zebras, elephants, gazelles, lions, giraffes and rhinos, and each friend was awestruck by the creatures observed.
>
> The first friend, Martin, commented boldly: "The Lord God has definitely created an amazing array of creatures that sing his praises and declare his glory to the ends of the earth, has he not?"
>
> The second friend, Charles, immediately responded: "An amazing array of creatures, to be sure. But you err, my good man, in ascribing their existence to a Creator. No, these incredible animals are the result of the unguided, purposeless combination of random mutation and natural selection. We too are the product of a natural evolutionary process. Indeed, we are no different from the creatures that we see."
>
> The third friend, Deepak, serenely replied: "I pray you both would be enlightened to the full reality disclosed by our brothers and sisters on the nature preserve. For they too bear the same spark of divinity that lies within you and me. Do you not sense them calling to you, seeking to communicate with your spirit? We are all potential gods and goddesses; we just need to awaken to our heightened state and take hold of the possibilities that lie before us."[2]

Martin, Charles, and Deepak saw the exact same animals in the exact same nature preserve. They experienced the same objective reality. Nevertheless, due to their vastly different worldviews, the three friends interpreted the experience differently. Why? Simply put, Martin, Charles, and Deepak are experiencing a clash of worldviews. Martin based his interpretation of the Serengeti on the authority of the Bible. Charles placed his interpretation on materialism, while Deepak based his on Hindu thought. They all saw the same thing with their physical eyes, but what they saw with the eyes of their minds and hearts was categorically distinct.

As the story indicates, different worldviews lead to vastly different interpretations of reality. C. S. Lewis writes, "The Christian and the Materialist hold different beliefs about the universe. They can't both be right. The one who is wrong will act in a way which simply doesn't fit the real universe."[3] In other words, the belief that the material world is all that exists and the belief that there is a spiritual world complete with angels and demons cannot both be right. In our story, Martin, Charles, and Deepak cannot all be right about the nature of reality.

Though modern culture pushes us to affirm any truth claim made by almost anyone, we cannot affirm both the conclusions of materialism and Christianity. They are contradictory. We cannot affirm both the Eastern spirituality of Hindu or Buddhist thought and materialism's denial of the spirit world. The spirit world either exists or it does not. If two worldviews totally oppose each other, only one can be true. Maybe neither view is true, but both definitely cannot correspond with reality.

We cannot affirm both the Eastern spirituality of Hindu or Buddhist thought and materialism's denial of the spirit world. The spirit world either exists or it does not.

Yet, our choice of a worldview should align with reality. According to Albert Einstein, "A man should look for what is, and not for what he thinks should be."[4] Just because we want something to be true does not mean it is true. Too often we can look for evidence to support our convictions instead of looking at the actual evidence and letting it lead to our convictions. A good detective does not decide who he thinks is guilty and then look for evidence to support his theory. A good detective collects the evidence and then follows that evidence to a conclusion.

Following a wrong worldview has horrible eternal consequences, and greatly reduces the effectiveness of our lives on earth. The way we see affects what we do and the ultimate outcome of our lives. We need the right prescription!

How Do You See It?

1. Modern culture often pushes us to affirm any truth claim made by almost anyone. Why is this a problem?

2. Why can we not affirm that both a secular materialist and a Hindu or Buddhist are correct about the nature of reality?

3. Why do you feel the "all paths lead to the top of the mountain" idea is so popular?

CHAPTER FOUR

EVERYBODY'S GOT FAITH

*"All worldviews begin with faith, a
metaphysical belief that cannot be
verified using scientific methods."*[1]
—Mary Poplin

F aith is part of everyday life. You go to a doctor whose name
you cannot pronounce. He gives you a prescription you
cannot read. You take it to a pharmacist you have never
seen. She gives you a medicine you do not understand, and yet
you take it anyway.[2]

People traditionally viewed as "religious"—i.e., Muslims,
Jews, Christians, Hindus, and Buddhists—are often referred to by
society as "people of faith." Most people readily acknowledge the
faith of Muslims, who trust in the Koran, the Hadith, and Islamic
teaching. Most people have no problem stating that Hindus have
faith in *karma*, reincarnation, the spirit world, and their religious
teachers. Few would dispute the assertion that Buddhists have

faith in the Noble Truths and that most Buddhists also believe in the spirit world, *karma*, and reincarnation. Not many challenge the idea that Christians have faith in Christ, Christ's resurrection, and the Bible.

Some who consider themselves "non-religious" push back on faith's role in their lives. Everyone has a worldview, though, and every worldview requires us to put faith in someone or something. We do not get to pick a "no faith" option in life. Every day we have to make choices that require faith—whether we like it or not, and whether we realize it or not.

Many secularists deny having faith. This is in spite of the secularists' strong faith in science, their own feelings, and their own experiences. Perhaps secularists have faith in *themselves* most of all.

Naturalists also demonstrate faith in several ways. Naturalists trust their own reason. They have faith in the scientific method and trust their own mind to make accurate conclusions. Yet, they also have faith in materialism which denies that our minds are more than a physical reality. Naturalists further have faith in evolution.

> We do not get to pick a "no faith" option in life. Every day we have to make choices that require faith—whether we like it or not, and whether we realize it or not.

Atheists also have a lot of faith. They have faith to believe there is no God. When many atheists encounter the reality of our finely tuned universe, they often have more faith to believe the fine tuning was caused by a multiverse, rather than by God's design. Atheists by faith also believe that logic, mathematical principles, and consciousness just happened by chance.

Allen Tennison notes that much of the faith of atheists is based on the premise that it is wrong to believe in the existence of anything without much evidence or a certain kind of evidence. This statement of faith is assumed to reach the conclusion that their lack of belief in God is on the basis of logic, not faith.[3]

Agnostics believe they cannot know for sure about the big questions of life. How do they know this? How can they be sure? Ultimately, agnostics need a lot of faith to believe agnosticism is true.

Even skeptics have faith—they need faith to believe that skepticism is true. University of California, Berkeley law professor Phillip Johnson rightly remarks, "One who claims to be a skeptic of one set of beliefs is actually a true believer in another set of beliefs."[4] In fact, skeptics who disbelieve one set of beliefs often have a lot of faith in the opposite set of beliefs.

Every action and thought we take is predicated on a belief we have. We sit on the chair because we believe it will hold us. We get on the plane because we believe it will take us to our destination. We choose to forgive our spouses because we believe they are sorry. We cannot even read this chapter and consider its ideas without believing our senses and our mind's ability to read the English language. We need faith to make sense of anything in the world.

"One who claims to be a skeptic of one set of beliefs is actually a true believer in another set of beliefs."
—Phillip Johnson

Every worldview requires us to have faith in someone or something. The real question is not, "Do you have faith?" but rather, "In whom or what do you ultimately believe?" The answer to this question is important because the type of faith we choose has consequences. Huge consequences. Eternal consequences. Your faith influences and shapes your worldview, which then influences and shapes your values and behavior.

Every worldview requires us to have faith in answering the big questions of life such as, "What is real?" or "How did the world begin?" Certain worldviews may give more evidence than others for their answers to these big questions, but all worldviews require us to take steps of faith toward what we see as being more reasonable. In what or whom have you placed your faith? Do you place your faith in your mind? Your abilities? Science and medicine? The government? Your family? Your understanding of consciousness?

Having faith in God and in the Bible is foundational for following Jesus Christ, but Christ followers do not see their faith as a "blind" faith. It is a reasonable faith given the evidence for the existence of God and for the reliability of His Word. Non-theists may claim to rely on evidence and facts—not faith—but they often dismiss certain types of evidence based on faith that such evidence is not permissible. They often ignore the faith they put in their thoughts, logic, the continued order of the universe, science, and even themselves.

Most non-theists struggle to explain the existence of the universe outside of chance. They may feel that chance is a reasonable explanation, but even this belief in chance requires faith to believe that something (the universe) came out of nothing by itself. Christ-followers and other theists often are just more honest and transparent about their faith than many non-theists. One might also say theists have faith *in* God, while non-theists choose faith *against* God.

How Do You See It?

1. Why can we not live without faith of some kind?

2. How does refusing faith in God affect the way we see the world? Why do so many refuse faith in God?

3. How does refusing faith in God affect our actions?

PART TWO:

Seeing God Clearly—
The Greatest Commandment

"But when the Pharisees heard that he had silenced the Sadducees, they gathered together. And one of them, a lawyer, asked him a question to test him. 'Teacher, which is the great commandment in the Law?' And he said to him, 'You shall love the Lord your God with all your heart and with all your soul and with all your mind. This is the great and first commandment.'"
Matthew 22:34-38

CHAPTER FIVE

THE GOD QUESTION

*"The most important element of any worldview is
what it says or does not say about God."[1]*
—Ronald Nash

Several years ago, *Encyclopedia Britannica* published a fifty-five-volume series entitled, *The Great Books of the Western World*. Mortimer Adler and his editorial team gathered the works of the best thinkers of the Western world, choosing books, essays, and poems that touch on the most important ideas that have been studied over the centuries, including ideas in law, science, philosophy, history, and theology. Readers can use the collection's index to investigate a particular topic and compare what various authors throughout the centuries have to say about it. Striking to the observant reader is the fact that the topic "God" receives the greatest number of pages in the volume series. When Adler was asked by a reviewer why the theme of God merited such extensive coverage, he answered, "Because more consequences for thought and action follow from the affirmation or denial of God than from answering any other basic question."[2]

In fact, the most critical component in anyone's worldview is whether that person believes in God or not. As Tim Keller says, "How we relate to God is the foundation of our thinking, because it determines the way we view the world."[3] Your belief in God's existence or non-existence will serve as the foundation on which all your analysis and interpretation of the world around you rests. People who believe that God exists form that conviction by faith, and this belief becomes the faith grid through which they view reality. Equally true is this: people who do not believe God exists also form their conviction by faith, and their conviction becomes the faith grid through which they understand and interpret reality. Whether we are aware of it or not, most of our analyses of the world around us proceed from our belief about God's existence. According to Keller, "You end up screening out all that does not fit with this view of life."[4]

Nearly every aspect of our worldview is impacted by our recognition or denial of the existence of God.

The importance of a person's view of God in how he or she sees the world cannot be overstated. Nearly every aspect of our worldview is impacted by our recognition or denial of the existence of God. There are significant differences between how theists (those who affirm the existence of God) and non-theists (those who deny His existence) view the world.

Most theists believe in a world beyond the material world, while non-theists deny the spirit world. Theists also believe in eternity in some sense, believing there is a dimension to which people go after their physical bodies stop functioning. Wide

26

varieties of beliefs about the afterlife exist, but belief in some sort of life after death is common with people who have some sort of God concept. Non-theists, on the other hand, typically deny any kind of life after death.

A person's belief in the existence of God also impacts how morality is viewed. Theists tend to acknowledge feeling some sort of moral concern for their actions while they are alive on earth, associating some type of reward or punishment with behavior, even if the reward is after they die. Non-theists often struggle to explain a logical basis for morality. Moral instincts exist, but why and are they valid?

Whether we acknowledge God or not impacts the way we see the world and how we live. Adam Kirsch shares:

> The best atheists agree with the best defenders of faith [in God] on one crucial point: that choice to believe or disbelieve is existentially the most important choice of all. It shapes one's whole understanding of human life and purpose, because it is a choice that each must make for him or herself.[5]

The first key then to understanding a person's worldview is to examine his or her answer to the question, "Does God exist?"

How Do You See It?

1. Why is your recognition of God or lack thereof the most important part of your worldview?

2. What major parts of our worldview are impacted by belief or disbelief in God?

3. How does one's belief in God affect medical decisions? The way we do business? The way we talk? The way we spend money and time?

CHAPTER SIX

WHAT IS GOD LIKE?

A lot of people think they know what God does not like, but have no idea of what He is like!

Y our worldview is impacted not only by what you believe about God's existence, but also by what you believe about His nature and character. A. W. Tozer, realizing how our theology of God impacts our worldview, writes, "What comes into our minds when we think about God is the most important thing about us."[1] Our understanding of God impacts how we relate with Him, what we expect from Him, and whether we even want to interact with Him. What we believe about God and how we relate with Him greatly impacts our self-understanding and our sense of purpose in life. Many people believe in God, but a belief in His existence does not equate to uniform belief in His nature.

Theists view God in a variety of ways. Animists see God as an inanimate power. Polytheists, such as most Hindus, believe in many gods that have many different attributes. Hindu pantheists further believe that humans themselves are deity. Many Buddhists are atheists, but others believe in multiple deities. As monotheists, Jews, Muslims, and Christians see God as being one, but one in different ways. Jews follow their traditions based on the Hebrew Scriptures. Muslims view Allah as an all-powerful Master. Christ followers see God as a Father revealed in the person of Jesus Christ whose Spirit lives within them. As you can see, the question "Do you believe God exists?" is not enough. To clarify a person's worldview, we must also ask, "In what kind of God do you believe?" Further, atheists should be asked, "What kind of God do you deny exists?"

"What comes into our minds when we think about God is the most important thing about us."
—A. W. Tozer

Christ followers acknowledge the many views of God in the world, but they also recognize that seeing well can only happen when they focus on how God has revealed himself in the Bible through Jesus Christ. In John 14, when Philip asks Jesus to show him the Father, Jesus replies, "Whoever has seen me has seen the Father" (v. 9b). The book of Hebrews explains, "He [Jesus] is the radiance of the glory of God and the exact imprint of His nature" (1:3). Jesus is a perfect representation of God! If we look to any other source for our understanding of God, we will miss out on Christ's truth and end up with a distorted understanding of God.

Ever since Adam and Eve lived in the Garden of Eden, the devil has tried to twist humanity's view of God. The father of lies convinced Adam and Eve that God did not have their best interests in mind and that He was keeping something good from them. Adam and Eve believed the lie, disobeyed God, felt shame, and then hid from God. Men and women have been hiding from

God ever since, and this is exactly what the enemy wants! The enemy desires to distort our view of God—to have us see God as holding out on us, loading us down with random rules, someone to be feared, someone who is untrustworthy, and yes, someone from whom to hide.

Ever since Adam and Eve lived in the Garden of Eden, the devil has tried to twist humanity's view of God.

How we see God absolutely affects our response to Him, and the devil knows this. If we view God as angry or vengeful, then we will run from Him and hide. When we see God as good, loving, and longing for relationship with us, we feel drawn to Him.

A twisted view of God will also impact how we interpret world events and God's hand in our circumstances. When we grasp God's heart for us, we love Him more. We want to obey His commands. We want to please Him. We do not blame Him whenever something bad happens. Rather, we run to Him for strength and comfort.

My mom was the most loving person I have ever known, yet she suffered a lot from mental illness. To a fault she would love people, even when some treated her poorly. Often while I was growing up and especially during the last ten years of her life, mental illness prevented Mom from being able to take care of herself.

Throughout my life I have wrestled with Mom's suffering and God's intentions for our family. Why did Mom have to go through the challenges she faced? Why was she not able to be fully present during many periods of my childhood, and why did she have to suffer the way she did the last ten years of her life?

I do not have an answer for Mom's suffering or the extra challenges I faced as I grew up at times without her support and care. I do *know* that God cared about Mom and our family. I do know He has worked some amazing, good things through her life, and I believe God has helped me to be a better person in some ways because of the challenges I faced.

At Mom's funeral I walked with my siblings into the church sanctuary as the song by Jenn Johnson and others, "Goodness of God," played. The chorus sounds, "All my life You have been faithful. All my life You have been so, so good. And as long as I am able, I will sing of the goodness of God!"[2] God is good in spite of things we do not understand on this side of heaven. We can trust His goodness even when we do not understand what we are experiencing. Never allow your suffering to mar your view of God. He is good. He is for you. He loves you forever.

How Do You See It?

1. A. W. Tozer said, "What comes into our minds when we think about God is the most important thing about us." What comes into your mind when you think about God?

2. Why does the enemy try so hard to distort our view of God?

3. Has your view of God been distorted by a particular circumstance in your life?

CHAPTER SEVEN

IS GOD AGAINST SEX?

*Like fire, sex is powerful but extremely
dangerous and destructive when
out of its intended boundaries.*

A s fallen humans, we often struggle with wanting our own
way. In our brokenness we desire things that go against
God's design and laws. When we understand His heart to
protect us, following rules He has given us makes more sense. Our
Creator knows us better than anyone else does. He designed us
and recognizes our strengths and vulnerabilities. The guidelines
God gives us in the Bible for our behavior are not to keep us from
fun, but to protect us and help us stay focused on His purposes.

For a season, my family and I lived in the mountains of India.
Many of the roads there have very narrow shoulders. To protect
travelers, the government constructs cement guard walls along
the twists and turns. In all my journeys there, I have never heard
anyone complain about the walls. I do not recall anyone acting

as if the walls were restricting them in their travel. No, instead of being viewed as killjoys, the walls were seen as protection from plunging several hundred, or even several thousand feet, down a mountain. God's guidelines act as guard walls that keep us from hurting ourselves and those we love. They are not meant to limit us, but to protect us.

The guidelines God gives us in the Bible for our behavior are not to keep us from fun, but to protect us and help us stay focused on His purposes.

Unfortunately, many still view the guidelines God has given us as limitations. One of the biggest lies the devil sells to humanity is that God's rules are designed to keep us from enjoying the good life. The truth is the exact opposite: God is a good Father who *always* has our best interests at heart. Jesus said He came that we might have abundant life (John 10:10). Our Maker knows how that abundant life can best happen.

One important guardrail God has constructed proclaims that sex is to be enjoyed within the boundary of marriage. In Western culture, perhaps no topic is more alluring than sex. Like fire, sex is powerful but extremely dangerous and destructive when out of its intended boundaries. God created sex as a spiritual, emotional, and physical activity. He designed sex for procreation but also for pleasure and bonding. Sex was created by God as a gift to be enjoyed within the covenant of marriage as He designed marriage, between one man and one woman. When we participate in sex in ways beyond God's design, we endanger ourselves and others.

Unfortunately, with his deceit and deception, the devil has drawn countless individuals over the guardrail that God designed for sexual intimacy. The devil entices people from safety with his lies: "Something that feels so good cannot be wrong," "You are committed in your hearts; that's more important than a piece of paper," and "How can expressing love hurt you?" He lies: "Sex has nothing to do with your relationship with God," "No one can say no to sex in today's culture," and "Everyone else is doing it, and nothing bad is happening to them." The biggest lie may be this one: "God is holding out on you—God does not want you to enjoy yourselves." It is an absolute lie of the enemy that God does not want us to enjoy sex. God created sex to be enjoyed by a man and woman within a marriage covenant. God does not want us to be hurt by having sex outside of His design.

Kylie[1] grew up in a Christ-honoring home and served Christ throughout her childhood and junior high years. In high school, she began charting her own path, which included a boyfriend named Zach. Kylie and Zach's relationship pushed past wise physical boundaries, and soon they were sleeping together. After her high school graduation, Kylie and Zach moved in together. She knew this went against God's Word, but it was what everyone else was doing, and she was afraid of losing Zach. Plus, having sex was fun.

Eleven years passed. Kylie still loved Zach, but her heart felt so empty. She was stressed and anxious, and nothing—alcohol, parties, sex, money, a good job—could fill the emptiness. Kylie also felt pain because now friends were getting married, and yet Zach saw no reason to get married or formalize their commitment to each other. Life was not turning out how she had dreamed.

At her job, Kylie began to spend more time with a gal named Lisa. Lisa radiated a joy and peace that Kylie desired to have in her own life. Lisa shared with Kylie about her faith in Christ and invited Kylie to attend a small group Bible study with her. As Kylie began hanging out with Lisa and her friends, Kylie realized that a relationship with Jesus was what she was missing. She recommitted her life to Christ and experienced peace she had not felt in a long time. However, she continued to live and sleep with

Zach. Kylie rationalized that Zach would soon be drawn to Christ by her example, that it would be too messy to move out (since they shared finances, furniture, and rent), and that God would forgive her since she loved Zach so much. Zach was even now talking about marriage.

She waited nearly a year, hoping Zach would ask her to marry him. It never happened. Zach said he was fine as things were, and if it wasn't enough for her, then she was free to move on. Kylie was heartbroken, but she realized that she wanted more. She wanted a husband who valued her and treasured her. She wanted the stability of building a home with a man who was committed to her and future children, who would put their needs and comforts above his own.

It was the hardest decision she ever made, but Kylie moved out of her and Zach's apartment. The months that followed were filled with terrible pain and grief, but as she clung to Jesus, she realized that she had never felt more valued, more treasured, or safer. One of Kylie's favorite worship songs is "Good, Good Father" by Chris Tomlin. Kylie says God has shown himself to be her good Father, who is restoring her and healing her heart and emotions. "I was so broken after Zach," she says. "I had used sex to get him to love me, but that was never the way God designed sex to be used. Sex was fun, but it always left me empty, because there was no commitment with it." When she realized she needed to stop sleeping with Zach, he said that God was "old school" and took the fun out of life. Kylie says, "Nothing could be further from the truth. God is not old-fashioned. He loves me and wants the best for me."

God is a good Father who wants us to be whole in Him. Sex was never designed to be our source of identity or primary place of pleasure. It is a gift, but like most gifts, it can be grossly abused. It can lead to addiction and great distraction from God's purposes.

We need God's help and guidance to enjoy sex in the way it was created to be enjoyed.

Sex was never designed to be our source of identity or primary place of pleasure. It is a gift, but like most gifts, it can be grossly abused.

Medical doctors Joe McIlhaney and Freda McKissic Bush make the bold claim that "the most up-to-date research suggests that most humans are 'designed' to be sexually monogamous with one mate for life."[2] Their research also shows that "the further individuals deviate from this behavior, the more problems they encounter, be they STDs, non-marital pregnancy, or emotional problems, including damaged ability to develop healthy connectedness with others, including future spouses."[3] God's design guards us from much harm!

God is for sex, but He gives guardrails for sex to protect people from harm and abuse. If you are a person who has suffered abuse, you probably appreciate the guardrails God has put in place even more than others. The Church's commitment to sexual morality is one reason it grew so quickly in the early centuries of Christianity, especially among women. In Roman society, wives had little status. Freeborn men married wives to obtain legal heirs, but it was culturally accepted that these men would seek sexual satisfaction with girlfriends, mistresses, prostitutes, other men, and, most of all, household slaves. A wife had to compete with a host of other people for her husband's love and attention.[4] God's standards of sexuality were welcomed by these first and second century women. Women were drawn to follow a God who gave rules that protected them, and slaves—both male and female— were also drawn to the Christian community. Living in constant fear of what their master might force them to do, they were drawn to Christ, who taught sexual purity and fidelity.

God is for sex, but He gives guardrails for sex to protect people from harm and abuse.

The abuse of sex does not change God's design. We need to be careful to view God's standards as safety precautions for our good. While the enemy twists the purpose of sex and promotes sexual immorality, God gives us safeguards to avoid the pain and even entrapment that accompany illicit sexual activity.

I remember one afternoon looking down the side of the mountain in North India at a car that had gone off the road and over the cliff. It was not a pretty sight. When we choose to question God's wisdom and treat His guidelines as restrictive rather than as protective, we end up in destructive thinking patterns, and we usually end up violating the guidelines. If we continue to accuse God of being a killjoy when He warns us of the dangers of sex outside marriage, we may go over the guardrail meant to protect us. If we ignore God's directions on sex before marriage, we will drive off a figurative cliff and face unnecessary shame and damage. Guardrails protect with our safety in mind.

How Do You See It?

1. Who do you know that has been hurt by sexual sin? Consider what lies led to their choices.

2. What are you doing to guard yourself from sexual sin?

3. What boundaries have you set to protect you and those you love?

CHAPTER EIGHT

DOES GOD CARE ABOUT SUFFERING?

*Our perception of God's
silence is not God's absence.*

Sex grabs society's attention, but perhaps the most common accusation against God's loving, good nature, and even His existence, is the problem of evil: if God is all-powerful and all-loving, then why does evil exist? God often gets blamed for the suffering or pain we see around us. Unfortunately, when we blame God, we end up distorting His character.

It is natural to ask questions when things are not the way we sense they should be. If God is real, loving, and all powerful, then why does He allow miscarriages, accidents, cancer, or abuse? Why does He permit rape, murder, and human trafficking to happen?

Volumes have been written on the problem of evil. As humans, we want answers that God does not always provide in the way we desire.

The reason we struggle with things we perceive as unjust or wrong is because we are made in God's image. As image bearers of the God who is fully just, we inwardly sense injustice. Our sense of right and wrong comes from God. C. S. Lewis in *Mere Christianity* notes,

> My argument against God was that the universe seemed so cruel and unjust. But how had I got this idea of just and unjust? A man does not call a line crooked unless he has some idea of a straight line. What was I comparing this universe with when I called it unjust?[1]

If we were just skin-covered robots without divine purpose, then we would not care about perceived wrongs, especially if they were to others and not to us. The longings we have for justice are evidence of being created by the One who defines justice and made us to be like Him.

If we were just skin-covered robots without divine purpose, then we would not care about perceived wrongs, especially if they were to others and not to us.

As we struggle with questions, pain, anger, and hurt, God wants us to come to Him. We do not have to censor our feelings when we talk with God. The biblical writers cry out with their questions and their pain. Habakkuk asks God, "O Lord, how long shall I cry for help, and you will not hear? Or cry to you 'Violence!' and you will not save?" (Hab 1:2). In his despair, Jeremiah cries, "Why does the way of the wicked prosper? Why do all who are treacherous thrive?" (Jer 12:1b). The Psalmist cries out, "Why have you forgotten me? Why do I go mourning because of the oppressions of the enemy? As with a deadly wound in my bones, my adversaries taunt me, while they say to me all the day long, 'Where is your God?'" (Ps 42:9-10). These men were upset about injustices they were seeing and experiencing, and they knew they could bring their pain and confusion to God.

God wants us to cry out to Him when we are in pain, when we feel angry, and when we are hurting. He hears our cries, and the remarkable thing is that He hurts and cries along with us. God is not an ambivalent watcher when we endure pain. He weeps with us and intercedes for us. The Psalmist says He keeps our tears in his bottle (Ps 56:8). God cares, and He walks with us through pain. He has promised to never leave us. The question is, though, will we stay with Him? Will we allow suffering to push us closer to God, or will we allow suffering to push us away from Him?

Will we allow suffering to push us closer to God, or will we allow suffering to push us away from Him?

Although never a Nazi Party member, Reinhard Bonnke's father served in the German Army during World War II. When Russian soldiers invaded Reinhard's homeland of Prussia, Reinhard's father was captured as a prisoner of war, and Reinhard's family was forced to flee their home. The atrocities of war impacted the whole Bonnke family, but Reinhard's older brothers viewed the suffering much differently than Reinhard. Reinhard did not understand why so many around them suffered, but he chose to keep his faith in God. Reinhard's brothers, on the other hand, became angry at God, questioning God's goodness and eventually turned away from God. Viewing him as the baby of the family, Reinhard's family did not expect him to become much in life. However, he became by far the most prominent in his family, seeing seventy-nine million people come to Christ through the gospel meetings he held. Reinhard's brothers eventually returned

41

to Christ, but they wasted many years ignoring God and being angry about what had happened during the war.

God wants to give us His perspective; as Keller writes, "Just because you can't see or imagine a good reason why God might allow something to happen doesn't mean there can't be one."[2] We make many assumptions in life that are incorrect because we cannot see everything God sees. If God were to give us His power for twenty-four hours, we would probably be tempted to change a number of things in our lives and even the world. However, if He were to give us His wisdom and perspective along with His power, we would likely leave many things as they are.

> "Just because you can't see or imagine a good
> reason why God might allow something to
> happen doesn't mean there can't be one."
> *—Tim Keller*

Corrie ten Boom's life teaches us much about suffering and our response to it. My wife travelled to Holland several years ago with her mom and sister, and top on their list of things to do was to tour the family home of Corrie ten Boom. Corrie and her family helped hundreds of Jews reach safety during the Nazi occupation of Holland. One day Corrie's family was betrayed. Soldiers ransacked the ten Boom home and arrested the family. Corrie and her sister, Betsie, were sent to a concentration camp, where Betsie eventually died. The suffering Corrie endured was unimaginable— beatings, strip searches, hard labor, fleas, starvation, the nauseating smell of human bodies being burned, and more. Corrie survived the horrors and was released from Ravensbruck twelve days after Betsie died and just before the war ended.

Today an embroidered crown hangs in the ten Boom family dining room. It is mounted with a glass backing so visitors can see both the front and back of the embroidered picture. Corrie would use this weaving when she shared about the experiences of her life. She would show people the underside of the embroidery, which was messy with all sorts of knots and crossed threads. From the backside a person could not tell what it was or even see a hint of the true beauty of the piece. When Corrie turned it over, though, there was a lovely crown, beautifully woven out of all those messy threads from the underside. Corrie taught that while we often only see the underside, God is the Master Weaver, and He will make something beautiful out of the tangled threads of our circumstances if we will allow Him. The crown hangs there as a reminder for all of us to look at our circumstances from God's perspective.

When asked why God does not stop the evil people in the world, apologist Frank Turek asks, "Suppose He starts with you?"[3] While the degree may vary, all of us have done something evil. Getting rid of evil would mean getting rid of us or turning us into robots. In other words, to stop evil, God would either have to wipe every human off the planet or take away humanity's ability to choose good or evil.

When asked why God does not stop the evil people in the world, apologist Frank Turek asks, "Suppose He starts with you?"

God gives people the freedom to make choices which have consequences in our world. That freedom allows for people to choose evil, but also love, joy and relationship. Do we really want God to remove our free will to stop us from sin? Besides, how do we know that God has not stopped evil? God likely has stopped a number of evil acts today, yet we ignore this because we are angry about the evil acts that did occur, the evil acts He did not stop. We want a world in which evil does not exist in any form, yet we also want our freedom.

During pain, followers of Christ need to remain careful about how they view God's character. God often gets blamed for things the enemy has done to us. The thief kills, steals, destroys (John 10:10), and then faults God. While it is rare for skeptics to thank God for the rain He sends on the just and the unjust, it is quite common for skeptics to blame God for the things they perceive as wrong. This is a double standard.

While it is rare for skeptics to thank God for the rain He sends on the just and the unjust, it is quite common for skeptics to blame God for the things they perceive as wrong. This is a double standard.

Some people point their fingers at God for the results of sin in our broken world. Others point their fingers at God when they are actually reaping the consequences of their own choices. When we see God as the cause of our pain and blame Him for our suffering, we are believing a lie. Our bad view of God will damage our intimacy with Him and affect our ability to see what He is doing and wants to do in our circumstances.

Our world is broken. Bad things do happen. In our lifetimes, we will all likely cry out to God, "Why don't you do something?" or "God, don't you care? I thought you loved me!" During those times, we must remember the Cross. God did take action against evil. The Cross is God's fullest response in the battle against evil and the evil one. On the Cross, Jesus went through the greatest level of pain anyone has ever experienced. He suffered unimaginable pain to prove His love for us and to win the ultimate battle over evil.

44

He suffered, and while sometimes we cannot say why such-and-such happened (you fill in the blank), we cannot say it is because Jesus does not care! In the midst of suffering, we must always remember Christ's monumental demonstration of love for us. He loved us then, and He loves us now. His love for us will never change!

How Do You See It?

1. How does the recognition of injustice point to God?

2. What are some responses to the question, "Why is there evil and suffering in the world?"

3. The devil uses suffering to cloud our vision. When we suffer, what should we remember and what does God want us to do?

CHAPTER NINE

WHAT ABOUT HELL?

"The doors of hell are locked on the inside."[1]
—C. S. Lewis

T he topic of hell is another way the enemy tries to distort people's vision of God. When the devil is not trying to convince humanity that hell is fiction, he tries to distort our view of God by blaming God for hell's horrific nature. The devil's common, accusatory question is as follows: "If God is truly loving, why would He send people to hell?"

Jesus, more than anyone else in the Bible, speaks about the reality of hell. He was obviously concerned that people took hell seriously. In Matthew alone, twelve separate passages record Jesus' teachings about hell and the eternal separation of nonbelievers from God.[2] Jesus also repeatedly emphasizes that this eternal separation from God is far worse than the physical pain and suffering here on earth.[3]

Though Jesus is clear about the reality of hell, nowhere in Scripture is there any indication that He desires people to go to there. Such a caricature of God's heart could not be more twisted. Second Peter 3:9 says, "The Lord is not slow to fulfill his promise as some count slowness, but is patient toward you, not wishing that any should perish, but that all should reach repentance." Second Timothy 2:4 proclaims that God wants all people to be saved and to come to the knowledge of the truth.

Though Jesus is clear about the reality of hell, nowhere in Scripture is there any indication that He desires people to go there.

Jesus said He came to earth that humanity might have abundant life (John 10:10). Abundant life is far different from hell! Portraying God as someone who desires people to go to hell is blasphemous. If that had been God's heart, He never would have sent Jesus to earth. Jesus never would have suffered the agony He experienced. He never would have given His life.

Part of humanity's pushback on the reality of hell stems from an unwillingness to acknowledge how sinful our lives are before we receive Christ's righteousness. No human is innocent. Humanity is hopelessly lost without Christ's intervention, but many humans defensively justify their own "goodness."

Contrary to Christian legalism and the beliefs of most world religions, no amount of doing good makes up for our sin. Islam teaches that if one's good deeds outweigh the bad, then one makes it into heaven. Hindu thought emphasizes doing good to gain good *karma*, which then overcomes bad *karma*. Yet neither the Koran nor Hindu scriptures make it clear how much good one must do to overcome one's bad deeds. How much good is enough to outweigh the bad?

The Bible certainly never promises forgiveness based on our works. In actuality, all our good deeds are like filthy rags (Isa 64:6). It is not by works of righteousness that we have done, but according to God's mercy that we are forgiven (Titus 3:5).

Jesus gave His life so all people can have their sins forgiven and their relationship with God restored. Unfortunately, many individuals refuse to acknowledge that they are neither innocent nor have they lived a "good" life. The Bible is clear that all have sinned and fallen short of God's glory (Rom 3:23). We are incapable of paying the price for even the "smallest" of sins we have committed. How then can we be "innocent" by our own works? Jesus said to the rich young ruler, "There is no one who is good, except God alone" (Mark 10:18, Luke 18:19). C. S. Lewis expresses it this way in *The Problem of Pain*: "Hell exists for those who refuse to acknowledge their guilt; therefore they can accept no forgiveness."[4]

Some may ask, "If God does not want anyone to go to hell, then why does hell exist?" Jesus said it was created for the devil and his angels (Matt 25:41). Hell was created to provide a place for the devil and his cohorts to stay apart from God and as a place for God's justice to be fully manifested on the enemy.

Why would anyone want to be in hell? Good question! Why does anyone want to be apart from God? Why do people ignore God while they live on earth? Why do people not want to relate with their Creator?

God's love for people necessitates hell because God never forces anyone to love or serve Him. Everyone has free will to have a relationship with God or not. It would have been immoral of God not to prepare a place for those who refuse to be with Him. If hell did not exist, where could those who want to avoid God live? Everything in heaven centers around God. To not have hell would be to force people to be around God, whom they resist. God allows people to choose. If people resist and spend their whole

49

lives not wanting to be with God on earth, will they suddenly want to spend eternity with Him? Relationship with God in heaven is for all who desire it, seek it, and want it. C. S. Lewis observes in *The Screwtape Letters*, "He [God] cannot ravish. He can only woo."[5]

Suppose a young man shows interest in a young lady. The lady, though, is not interested in a romantic relationship with the young man and clearly communicates the same to the man. What is the most loving thing the man can do? Leave her alone. That is what God does with those who refuse Him. He leaves them alone to their desires. God never forces himself on anyone.

C. S. Lewis puts it like this: "The doors of hell are locked on the inside."[6] People lock the door on God and choose to be apart from Him. They choose hell. God does not want anyone to go there. Yet, God is too good to make people live with Him in heaven. He does not coerce people to live in His presence forever.

With His life and death on the Cross, Jesus essentially says, "You can go to hell over my dead body." Many unfortunately choose to do just that—to walk over Christ's body and ignore Christ's love. They ignore the great price Christ paid to have a relationship with them.

The fairness and justness of God exist beyond our human comprehension. God defines justice. Those who land in heaven and those who land in hell will not have any grounds to complain about being treated unfairly. C. S. Lewis writes in *The Great Divorce*, "There are only two kinds of people in the end: those who say to God, 'Thy will be done,' and those to whom God says, in the end, 'Thy will be done.'"[7]

To those who continue to criticize God in regard to hell, Lewis speaks again:

> In the long run the answer to all those who object to the doctrine of hell is itself a question: "What are you asking God to do?" To wipe out their past sins and, at all costs, to give

them a fresh start, smoothing every difficulty and offering every miraculous help? But he has done so, on Calvary. To forgive them? They will not be forgiven. To leave them alone? Alas, I am afraid that is what he does.[8] [Lewis is referring to an unrepentant person who has died.]

People send themselves to hell. The Apostle Paul describes people who have shut God out of their lives: "Although they knew God, they did not honor Him as God or give thanks to Him, but they became futile in their thinking, and their senseless minds were darkened. Claiming to be wise, they became fools" (Rom 1:21-22). Paul again and again uses a certain phrase for God's response to this situation: "Therefore God gave them up to sinful desires" (v. 24), "And for this reason God gave them up to degrading passions" (v. 26), "And since they did not see fit to acknowledge God, God gave them up to a debased mind to do things that should not be done" (v. 28).

What's the phrase that keeps coming up? God gave them up. Human freedom means freedom to choose hell—the logical outcome of living one's life apart from God. It is the result of repeatedly choosing to be self-centered rather than God-centered. Keller connects this self-centeredness with its consequences:

A common image of hell in the Bible is that of fire. Fire disintegrates. Even in this life we can see the kind of soul disintegration that self-centeredness creates. We know how selfishness and self-absorption leads to piercing bitterness, nauseating envy, paralyzing anxiety, paranoid thoughts, and the mental denials and distortions that accompany them. Now ask the question: "What if when we die we don't end, but spiritually our life extends on into eternity?" Hell, then, is the trajectory of the soul, living a self-absorbed, self-centered life, going on and on forever.[9]

We must view God's heart toward people through the lens of John 3:16, which says, "God so loved the world that He gave His only Son that whoever believes in Him should not perish, but have everlasting life." God loves people and has paid the ultimate price so all people may relate with Him as their Father. May we do our best to proclaim this good news!

How Do You See It?

1. Hell is horrible, yet real. Why does it exist?

2. What Bible verses clearly indicate Jesus does not want anyone to be in hell?

3. Why would it be wrong for God to force people to be with Him?

CHAPTER TEN

THE BETTER WE SEE HIM, THE MORE WE LOVE HIM

"I don't pray because I'm into prayer.
I pray because I'm into Jesus."[1]
—Pete Greig

Seeing God clearly impacts everything we do, including the greatest thing we do: loving Him. In Matthew 22:37 Jesus emphasizes we are to love God with our whole heart, mind and strength. This is our greatest "work" or "job" as God's people, and it flows quite naturally as we see God well.

When we avoid misconceptions about God, we love Him better. Seeing God as a capricious lawgiver who wants to limit my options in life will lead to less passion toward Him. Believing that God is trying to exclude people from spending eternity with Him will affect my love for Him. If I feel that the suffering I endure is capriciously caused by God, my love for Him will further be impacted.

A. W. Tozer writes, "We are called to an everlasting preoccupation with God."[2] He is our treasure, and our whole being must yearn for Him. Loving God with our hearts, our souls, and our minds emphasizes that we should love God with every part of who we are.

"We are called to an everlasting preoccupation with God."
–A. W. Tozer

As we conclude this section on the Greatest Commandment, we want to address the question, "How do we love God?" Loving Him is the most important thing we do, so we want to do it well. We want to love Him as best we can.

How Do We Love God?
We Pay Attention to Him.

As we see God clearly, we will pay more attention to Him. We will want Him to be a part of every part of our lives. Why would we not pay attention to someone who loves us more than anyone else? Why would we not want to ask questions from the One who knows everything? Why would we not run to the source of all comfort when we are in pain? When we have a need, why not reach out to Jehovah-Jireh, our provider?

We give our attention to God not just because He can meet our needs but also because we respond to His kindness, which leads us to repentance (Rom 2:4). Our hearts burn within us when we walk with Him (Luke 24:32). We recognize that He is God, and He is LORD over all.

Why would we ignore God? Idolatry is a primary reason. One of the first signs that we may have an idol in our lives is a lukewarm feeling in our love toward God. Something or someone distracts our attention from God. We love something or someone more than we love God. St. John of the Cross notes, "Any thought not centered on God is stolen from Him."[3] God deserves our attention. We show Him our love by centering our thoughts on Him.

Generally, couples do not get engaged simply because they want to enjoy the marriage ceremony. They want to live life together. They want to be an ongoing part of each other's lives. Likewise, loving God is not something we do only during ceremonies or only on certain days of the week. Our love for God must lead to a consistent walk with Him.

In the seventeenth century, a Carmelite friar named Brother Lawrence wrote a spiritual classic, *The Practice of the Presence of God*. Brother Lawrence's life goal was to live in the presence of God. His life was an experiment in how to constantly pay attention to God and live in continual communion with Christ. Brother Lawrence believed that prayer is not necessarily "saying prayers" but "a way of living in which all we do becomes a prayer." His life demonstrated the importance of seeing God and continually paying attention to Him.

To love God, we must pay attention to Him. People give time to the ones they love. How much more should those who love God pay attention to Him and acknowledge Him throughout their lives?

How Do We Love God?
We Obey Him.

A second way we outwardly demonstrate our love for God is through our obedience to Him. Jesus said if we love Him, we will keep His commands (John 14:15). He further says in John 14, "Whoever has my commandments and keeps them, he it is who loves me" (v. 21a).

If we find we are having a hard time obeying God, it may be because we have a faulty view of who He is. As we see God more clearly, our love for Him increases, and we want to obey Him more. We understand that His commands are not burdensome (1 John 5:3).

When we love someone, we do things for that person that we would never dream of doing for others. Jacob worked seven years to marry Rachel, but Genesis says that the years flew by quickly because of his great love for her (Gen 29:20). Love for God motivates us to obey Him in even difficult circumstances.

A primary part of loving God and demonstrating obedience is saying "yes" to whatever part God wants us to play in His story. Life is not meant to center around ourselves but rather around God's story and plan for our lives.

As humans we tend to focus on ourselves and see ourselves as the main character in the story of our lives. This is especially common in Western cultures, which emphasize individualism. In most Western cultures, focusing on oneself is as natural as breathing air.

When we as individuals look at a group picture, whom do we tend to look for first? Ourselves! We tend to wonder, "How do I look?" "What kind of impression will this picture give to others?" "Did the picture capture me well?" Without thought, we often only consider how life's events affect our lives, or maybe our family's lives, if we are considerate. Yet much more important is how our lives fit into God's eternal, grand plan.

Maps at indoor shopping malls can help us grasp how we are just one part of a much bigger story, the Story of God. When we look at a map at a kiosk in the mall, we typically see the layout of the entire complex. We see the bigger picture. We might be looking for a particular store on the map, but the map also reveals another key piece of information: the "You are here" marker. By seeing the whole mall on the map with all its different stores, as well as where we are located, we get a better sense of how our location fits in with the bigger picture. We can also see where we need to go next.

We need God to show us the big map of His story and how we fit in the larger context. This rarely happens instantaneously, but God is faithful to reveal to us more and more as we grow in our understanding about His plan. Little by little, step by step, we grasp the purpose God has assigned to us.

How Do You See It?

1. What is something you have recently learned about God that causes you to love Him more?

2. According to Tozer, "We are called to an everlasting preoccupation with God."[4] Taking an honest look at your life, what are you most preoccupied with right now?

3. Of the two ways to demonstrate love to God—paying attention to Him and obeying Him—which do you find harder? Why?

PART THREE:

Seeing People Clearly—
The Second Greatest
Commandment

*"And a second is like it: You shall love your
neighbor as yourself. On these two commandments
depend all the Law and the Prophets."*
Matthew 22:39-40

CHAPTER ELEVEN

THE IMMENSE VALUE OF HUMAN LIFE

*"There are no ordinary people. You have
never talked to a mere mortal."*[1]
—C. S. Lewis

After our view of God, how we view people is the most
critical parts of our worldview. Jesus intentionally places
loving God as the Greatest Commandment in part because
of the motivation, strength, and guidance we need from God to
obey the *second* Greatest Commandment—loving others as we
love ourselves. To obey the second Greatest Commandment, we
need to see people from God's perspective. We need God's help!

Humans are naturally self-centered. We do not naturally love
others as ourselves. It is only as we surrender our lives to God and

ask Him to work in our life that God can give us the capacity and the desire to love our neighbors as ourselves (Matt 22:39).

Prioritizing God is essential to seeing people well. We need His assistance to overcome stereotypes, prejudices, biases, and cultural differences as we view people. We need His strength to love even our enemies and to see the value God has placed in their lives.

Seeing the Value of Human Life

Thaddeus[2] is a sixty-some-year-old man who lives in our neighborhood. His facial shape is distinct, tied to a syndrome that limits Thaddeus' cognitive abilities. Just about every day Thaddeus can be seen walking around North Central University (NCU) and the park next to campus, looking for someone to talk to. Thaddeus' ability to "produce" in our world is limited, yet whenever he visits the campus of NCU he receives greeting after greeting. The students love Thaddeus. A few years ago, Thaddeus was hit by a car while walking around the neighborhood. He was rushed to the hospital, and a great outpouring of prayers and love ensued. NCU students even bought Thaddeus a new coat with reflective markers on it to make him more visible to motorists as he walks through our area. Why did the students react as they did? Because they understand that while Thaddeus is much older than any of them and much lower in his intellectual abilities, he is made in God's image. Thaddeus' life, like all human life, is sacred.

Anyone who follows a biblical worldview sees the value of human life. From the beginning, God makes it clear in His Word that people have intrinsic value. In Genesis 1:26-27 God says,

> Let us make man in our image, after our likeness, and let them have dominion over the fish of the sea and over the birds of the heavens and over the livestock and over all the earth and over every creeping thing that creeps on the earth. So God created man in his own image, in the image of God he created him; male and female he created them.

People were created differently than animals. People were made in God's image, and thus they have enormous innate value.

Emphasis on men and women being created in God's image continues in Genesis even after the Fall. At the beginning of Genesis 5, as the genealogies are about to start, humanity is again freshly identified as being created in God's image. Then early in Genesis 9, right after the flood wipes out virtually all of the human race, God reminds Noah and his family that people have been made in the image of God. God tells Noah, "I will demand an accounting for the life of another human being" (9:5). God's justification for the serious punishment that murder warrants directly connects with humanity's creation in God's image. Even in their fallen state, all humans carry the image of God.

Creation in God's image indicates both a special connection with God and an intended reflection of God. John Kilner understands that this connection with God is the basis of human dignity:

> All of humanity participates in human dignity. All of humanity is offered human destiny, though only some embrace and will experience it. Christ and humanity, connection and reflection, dignity and destiny—these lie at the heart of what God's image is all about.[3]

Humans connect with God and reflect His nature in ways that other parts of creation cannot.

First, *humans are the crown of God's creation on earth.* Scripture records nothing else as being created in God's image. Jesus himself indicates that humans have far more value than animals. In Matthew 12:12, Jesus says, "Of how much more value is a man than a sheep!" In Luke 13:15-16, Jesus answers the ruler of the synagogue who was indignant because Jesus healed someone on the Sabbath:

> You hypocrites! Does not each of you on the Sabbath untie his ox or his donkey from the manger and lead it away to water it? And ought not this woman, a daughter of Abraham

whom Satan bound for eighteen years, be loosed from this bond on the Sabbath day?[4]

Second, *humans can relate with God in ways animals cannot*. Yes, animals do relate with God as their Creator, and they are capable of being loved, but humans have a much deeper relationship with God. We have example after example of humans personally interacting with God. Before the Fall, the first humans (Adam and Eve) interacted with God in the Garden of Eden, walking and talking with Him (Gen 3:9-13). Genesis records numerous conversations between Abraham and God (12:1-3; 15; 17), including one in which Abraham pleads for Sodom (18:16-31). Exodus 33:11 shares that God spoke to Moses "face to face, as one speaks to a friend." In the New Testament, many people personally encountered God through Jesus. Jesus related to fishermen, tax collectors, Pharisees, and prostitutes. He spoke with Jews, Samaritans, Greeks, and Romans. He attended weddings and cried at funerals. From Genesis to Revelation, the Bible records men and women enjoying relationship with God.

"Of how much more value is a man than a sheep!"
—Jesus (Matt 12:12)

Third, *humans have the capacity to speak and act on God's behalf*. God gave humans dominion over the earth, commanding them to "Rule over the fish of the sea and the birds of the air and over every living creature that moves on the ground" (Gen 1:28-30). God brought the animals to Adam so he could name them (2:19-20). Throughout the Bible, prophets spoke on God's behalf and also acted on His behalf. Elijah, Elisha, Ezekiel, Jeremiah, and Agabus are just some of the prophets God used to speak on His behalf. Connected with this capacity to speak for God is the mandate given in the Great Commission to disciple all nations (Matt 28:18-20). Jesus commissioned believers to act in His authority and to spread the Kingdom of God everywhere. (Please see *Part Four, Seeing Our Assignment—The Great Commission—Clearly*.)

Being made in God's image makes humans unique. James Sire observes:

> [W]e can summarize this conception of humankind in God's image by saying that, like God, we have personality, self-transcendence, intelligence (the capacity for reason and knowledge), morality (the capacity for recognizing and understanding good and evil), gregariousness or social capacity (our characteristic and fundamental desire and need for human companionship—community—especially represented by the 'male and female' aspect) and creativity (the ability to imagine new things or to endow old things with new significance).[5]

All the characteristics Sire mentions differentiate humans from animals. God has uniquely made humans in His image to reflect Him.

The high value that a biblical worldview places on humans contrasts sharply with other worldviews. Naturalism and its common counterpart, materialism, are common to the worldviews of skeptics, atheists, and secularists. Materialism asserts that everything is matter and dependent on physical processes. Naturalism also asserts that everything is dependent on physical processes. Both deny the supernatural, and both consequently also deny humanity's creation in the image of God.

Removing humanity's status as an image-bearer of God strips humans of dignity, reducing their status to that of animals. Ingrid Newkirk, co-founder of People for the Ethical Treatment of Animals (PETA), expounds on materialistic ethics, saying, "There is no rational reason for saying that a human being has special rights. A rat is a pig is a dog is a boy."[6]

Moving to the opposite end of the spectrum, pantheistic Hindu traditions believe people to be gods, which is quite a lofty understanding of humankind. Hindus, however, are also part of a caste system, which assigns value at birth according to where a person is located in the caste hierarchy. So, on one hand, Hindu pantheism values people highly, but on the other hand, people's value is quite dependent upon their castes (with animals being an even lower part of the whole system). Part of the *dharma* (duty) of lower castes is to do enough good works to graduate to the next caste level. Hindus may even be discouraged from showing compassion toward others, as it may interfere with the other person paying for mistakes made in past lives and earning his or her own way to a higher caste level in the next life.

While they both teach wrong views of humanity, there is a strong contrast between materialism and pantheism. Materialism reduces us to nothing more than a thinking machine, while pantheism deludes us into an inflated sense of our own identity. One reduces a human's dignity and value, while the other is self-deifying. Neither extreme is accurate.

Alan Johnson, missionary to Thailand, provides some insight about how Buddhists view humans, especially in comparison to other living beings. Johnson was reading Luke 5 to Thai students learning English. This passage records the miraculous catch of fish and Jesus' calling Peter to discipleship. After reading the story in English, Alan switched to discussing the story in the Thai language in order to check his students' understanding. He began by asking some simple questions:

"Who is the story about?"

After a brief discussion among themselves, they answered, "Jesus."

"Who else is in the story?"

Again, they discussed before answering, "Peter."

"Where did the story take place?"

"By the lake," they answered, after discussing their response.

Then Alan asked, "Why did Peter say, 'Go away from me, I am a sinful man'?"

This time there was no discussion among the students. One immediately and confidently answered, "Because he had killed all those fish."[7]

The Thai students assumed Peter to be sinful because killing another sentient being is against a Buddhist precept. In a Buddhist worldview, all living, sentient beings are on journeys of reincarnation to enlightenment. Insects, animals, demons, and humans are all journeying together. Humans lose some of their uniqueness as they like insects and demons are fellow travelers. In Buddhist thought, humans are definitely not seen and valued as unique image bearers of the one, true God.

Islamic theology sees humans as creations of God who relate to God as slaves or servants relate to their master. "Islam" means "submission," so the trend within Islamic theology of humans submitting to God is consistent with its name. Christianity also acknowledges God as Creator and also recognizes humanity's role as slaves or servants, but Jesus also emphasized sonship (Matt 6:9). The Bible clearly states sonship is the primary relationship believers have with God (Gal 4:7). Islam forbids looking to God as a Father.

To illustrate the great love God has for us as His image-bearers, Barbara Johnson shares a story about a woman who was dying. A priest was summoned, and he attempted to comfort the woman, but to no avail.

> "I have wasted my life," she said. "I have ruined my life and every life around me. Now I am dying. There is no hope for me."
>
> The priest saw a framed picture of a pretty girl on the dresser. "Who is this?" he asked.

The woman brightened. "She's my daughter, the one beautiful thing in my life."

"And would you help her if she were in trouble or made a mistake? Would you forgive her? Would you still love her?"

"Of course I would!" cried the woman. "I would do anything for her! Why do you ask such a question?"

"Because I want you to know," said the priest, "that God has a picture of you on his dresser."[8]

God may not have literal pictures of humans on His dresser (God does not need a dresser!), but more than words could ever express, humans matter to God. Isaiah tells us that God has our names engraved upon His hands (Isa 49:16). As a mother cannot forget her nursing baby, He cannot forget us (Isa 49:15). God has created humans as children in His image, and He never forgets us! People matter to God!

How Do You See It?

1. Why do you think God wants us to love Him first and then others as ourselves?

2. As humans, we love our animal pets, yet we know we are different than them. How are animals different from people, and why is it important to keep this distinction?

3. How do humans connect with God and reflect God's nature in ways other parts of creation cannot?

4. How does a biblical view of being made in God's image contrast with a materialistic or pantheistic view of people?

CHAPTER TWELVE

HOW OUR VIEW OF PEOPLE IMPACTS HOW WE TREAT THEM

*"Whoever oppresses a poor man
insults his Maker."*
Proverbs 14:31

Viktor Frankl spent several years in a Nazi death camp, but instead of blaming God for the Holocaust, he blamed all of its horror on people who truly lived out their atheistic worldviews. In his book, *The Doctor and the Soul*, Frankl says:

> If we present a man with a concept of man which is not true, we may well corrupt him. When we present man as an automaton

of reflexes, as a mind-machine, as a bundle of instincts, as a pawn of drives and reactions, as a mere product of instinct, heredity, and environment, we feed the nihilism to which modern man is, in any case, prone. I became acquainted with the last stage of that corruption in my second concentration camp, Auschwitz. The gas chambers of Auschwitz were the ultimate consequence of the theory that man is nothing but the product of heredity and environment—or, as the Nazi liked to say, of "Blood and Soil." I am absolutely convinced that the gas chambers of Auschwitz, Treblinka, and Maidanek were ultimately prepared not in some Ministry or other in Berlin, but rather at the desks and in the lecture halls of nihilistic scientists and philosophers.[1]

Our worldview strongly impacts the way we see people and the value we place upon them, which inevitably effects the way we treat them. Dietrich von Hildebrand recognized that it was precisely the biblical teaching that all humanity continues in the undeformed image of God that offered the greatest defense against Hitler's destructive initiatives. Soon after being forced to flee Nazi Germany in 1933, von Hildebrand wrote: "All of Western Christian civilization stands and falls with the words of Genesis, 'God made man in His image.'"[2] If only Hitler would have recognized the image of God in the Jews and disabled people who did not meet his standard.

Too often when we see people, we are like the blind man in Mark 8. At Bethsaida some people brought Jesus a blind man and begged Jesus to heal him. Jesus spit on the man's eyes, laid hands on him, and then asked the blind man, "Do you see anything?" The blind man looked up and said, "I see people, *but they look like trees, walking*" [italics added]. Then Jesus laid His hands on the man's eyes again, and the man's sight was fully restored, and he saw everything clearly (vv. 22-26).

Sometimes we too are blind. Sometimes we see people as objects, *as trees walking*, rather than as creations made in the image of God and valuable to Him. We need Jesus to open our eyes!

Jesus is our best example of seeing value in people. He saw people differently than others did and consequently treated people differently, lavishing them with love and respect. Though lepers were outcasts in Jesus' day, He saw them as valuable and touched them (Mark 1:41). While Jewish culture did not esteem women highly, Jesus saw women as valuable, recognizing their importance and talking with them (John 4:7-30). Jesus even saw the value in tax collectors, eating with them and inviting them to follow Him (Luke 19:1-20). Whether they were rich or poor, healthy or sick, male or female, Jesus treated all people with love and respect.

Sometimes we see people as objects, as trees walking, rather than as creations made in the image of God and valuable to Him.

Jesus saw great value in people in spite of the damage sin had caused in the world and in the lives of the individuals He met. Much has been written about God's image in humanity being marred in some way through sin. Certainly, humanity was disfigured when Adam and Eve sinned. Romans 5 says much about this, emphasizing how the sin of Adam led to the spiritual death of all. Yet, Jesus still recognized the value of all humans He encountered, in spite of their sinful nature inherited from Adam and Eve. Although the image of God in humanity was damaged by sin, humanity's great value still remains. Otherwise, Jesus would not have given His life in exchange for them!

Throughout history, Christians have also seen the value of people, and perhaps nowhere is this demonstrated more clearly than in the area of healthcare. The Early Church recognized the value of sick people and cared for them, while the surrounding Roman and Greek culture did not. Gary Ferngren writes: "The

71

classical world possessed no religious or philosophical basis for the concept of the divine dignity of human persons, and without such support, the right to live was granted or withheld by family or society almost at a whim."[3] Christians who followed a God that commanded them to "Love thy neighbor as thyself" could not be whimsical about their care for others.

> ## "The classical world possessed no religious or philosophical basis for the concept of the divine dignity of human persons, and without such support, the right to live was granted or withheld by family or society almost at a whim."
> *—Gary Ferngren*

Belief in the value of humans led early Christ followers to refuse to participate in the common practice of infanticide. Deformed or unwanted children were frequently left outdoors to die. Christ followers adopted many of these children and gained a reputation for such in the Roman Empire.[4]

Since the Church began, Christ followers have cared for the sick during plagues. In the Antonine Plague (AD 165-180) and Plague of Cyprian (AD 249-262), Christ followers cared for the victims, whether the victims were following Christ or not. Many years later Martin Luther and his pregnant wife, along with other Christians, cared for the sick during the Black Death in Europe.[5]

Christ followers have pioneered much in healthcare because of the truth that all people matter to God. Once the Christian faith became the official religion of the Roman Empire, healthcare ministry expanded considerably. The Council of Nicea (AD 325) commissioned bishops to establish hospice care in every city where a church building existed. The first hospital was built under

St. Basil in Caesarea (AD 369). By the Middle Ages, hospitals existed throughout Europe.[6]

Viewing slaves and criminals as God's image-bearers further led Christ followers to oppose Roman gladiatorial games. These brutal games killed many and were outlawed in the late fourth century in the East and the early fifth century in the West. Telemachus, a Christian monk, is credited with stopping these atrocities. Telemachus came from the Roman countryside to the city to encourage the churches in their faith. While in town he saw the crowds filling the Coliseum and followed them, curious as to what might unfold. What Telemachus witnessed broke his heart.

Wearing colorful body armor, gladiators marched around the perimeter of the battlefield, raising their weapons of choice. After completing this display of strength, the gladiators stood in the presence of the emperor and shouted, "Hail, Caesar, those about to die salute thee!"

The combat ensued, with the gladiators stabbing their opponents until they lay defenseless on the ground. When his opponent was subdued, a gladiator would cry out to the crowd, asking if he should finish his opponent or spare him. If a thumbs down was given by the crowd, the conquered was slain on the spot.

Telemachus was stunned by the cruelty that so many jaded Romans had accepted as the status quo. Motivated by the knowledge that all people are made in the image of God, Telemachus did the unthinkable: He jumped from the stands onto the field and placed himself between two gladiators. Clad only in a hermit's robe and armed only with a passion for God, Telemachus challenged the gladiators to cease their shedding of blood and the taking of life. The crowd and the gladiators were enraged at Telemachus' meddling in their games. One of the gladiators stabbed Telemachus, killing him in front of the crowd.

History records that Telemachus' death was not in vain. Something about witnessing the murder of this holy man sent shockwaves through the auditorium. God used the zeal and courage of one man to change the course of history. How? The Romans abandoned their gladiator games from that day forward. The Christian Emperor Honorius, so impressed by Telemachus' martyrdom, issued a historic ban on gladiatorial fights. The last known gladiatorial fight in Rome was on January 1, AD 404.[7]

While gladiator games were limited in their location and duration, slavery has had a long, terrible worldwide history. However, it has been Christ followers who have led the way in abolishing it. Rodney Stark notes that of all the world's religions, including the three great monotheisms, only in Christianity did the idea develop that slavery was sinful and must be abolished.[8] The biblical belief that all people are created in God's image compelled Christ followers to lead the fight.

"Of all the world's religions, including the three great monotheisms, only in Christianity did the idea develop that slavery was sinful and must be abolished."
–Rodney Stark

Antislavery doctrines began to appear in Christian theology soon after the decline of Rome.[9] Gregory of Nyssa, the younger brother of Basil the Great, is often referred to as the first abolitionist. In the fourth century in his fourth homily (sermon) on Ecclesiastes, Gregory denounced the practice of Christians owning slaves based on his conviction of all humans being made in the image of God.[10] In the fifth century, Saint Patrick's letter to the Soldiers of Coroticus condemning the enslavement of the Irish was another Christian anti-slavery document.[11] Later in the seventh century, Saint Bathilde (wife of King Clovis II) became famous for her campaign to stop slavery. In AD 851 Saint Anskar began his efforts to halt the Viking slave trade.[12]

By the Middle Ages, Europe's cultural view of humanity had so been influenced by the Bible that slavery died out in Christian Europe in all but the fringes.[13] In the thirteenth century, Saint Thomas Aquinas had deduced that slavery was a sin, and a series of popes upheld his position, beginning in 1435 and culminating in three major pronouncements against slavery by Pope Paul III in 1537.[14] When Europeans subsequently instituted slavery in the New World, they did so over strong papal opposition and many other Christian voices who opposed it.

Slavery was a horrible part of America's early history. Even Christians in Southern states practiced slavery, and today America is still reaping the evil consequences sown by the seed of slavery. When we do not honor the value God has placed on people, we dishonor Him and bring harm to society.

Although in America many Christ followers in the South did not stand against slavery, there were many Christ followers who did. Just as believers worldwide led the way throughout history in the fight against slavery, so also in America Christ followers led the charge to eradicate slavery from the country. Recognizing that all people, regardless of the color of their skin, carried the image of God, churches and local congregations issued official statements against slavery. The abolitionists spoke almost exclusively in the language of Christian faith, and although many Southern clergy proposed theological defenses of slavery (some even denying the humanity of slaves), pro-slavery rhetoric was overwhelmingly secular. References were made to "liberty" and "states' rights," not to "sin" or "salvation."[15]

The Quakers, a Christian group, perceived the image of God in slaves and led the early fight in America against slavery. One of their leaders, John Woolman, devoted his life to spreading the message of abolition, which he based exclusively on biblical objections.[16] Anthony Benezet, whose family were French Protestants, worked with the Quakers in founding an anti-slavery society in America.[17] This society, The Pennsylvania Society for Promoting the Abolition of Slavery (PAS), founded in 1775, was the world's first antislavery society.[18]

Abolitionists like Sojourner Truth saw the value of black Americans and correctly appealed to the Bible as they pressed for the freedom of slaves. Perhaps Truth's love of Christ and fight for equality is best summed up by her own words:

> Children, who made your skin white? Was it not God? Who made mine black? Was it not the same God? Am I to blame, therefore, because my skin is black? ... Does not God love colored children as well as white children? And did not the same Savior die to save the one as well as the other?[19]

British Quakers gained enthusiasm for abolition from their American cousins, and they too provided the initial biblical backbone of the antislavery movement.[20] British missionary David Livingstone's journals stirred up outcry in Europe against slavery. He estimated that 80,000 slaves died each year in Africa as they were being transported by Muslim slave traders from interior Africa to coasts such as Zanzibar. He referred to Muslim slave trade in Africa as "a monster brooding over Africa" and estimated that "not even one tenth arrive at their destination."[21]

The last letter John Wesley wrote six days before his death was to William Wilberforce, urging him to persevere to the end in his fight against slavery, that "execrable sum of all villainies."[22] Wilberforce did endure, devoting most of his life to seeing the slave trade abolished in the United Kingdom. Slavery in the British Empire was abolished days after Wilberforce died.[23]

Humanity's creation in God's image has also inspired initiatives to overcome the oppression of Native Americans. The Spanish colonization of the West Indies and other areas of the Americas during the sixteenth century provides an excellent illustration. In the face of much oppression, many Spanish friars risked their lives for the benefit of indigenous people. Their motivation was simply "the abiding confidence that they would not encounter any human being in any rural compound or village or city who was not created in the image and likeness of the God and Father of Jesus Christ."[24]

Christ followers have also led the way in promoting the value of women. We have noted earlier in this chapter that Jesus' honoring of women far exceeded the cultural and religious norms of His day. Though it was common in the Greco-Roman world to throw out new female infants to die from exposure, the Church forbid its members to do so. Greco-Roman society devalued unmarried women, and Augustus made it illegal for a widow to go more than two years without remarrying. Christ followers did not force widows to marry, though, and supported widows financially so they were not under great pressure to remarry. Pagan widows lost all control of their husband's estate when they remarried, but the Church allowed widows to maintain their husband's estate. Furthermore, Christ followers did not believe in cohabitation. If a male disciple of Christ wanted to live with a woman, he had to marry her; this gave women far greater security. The Church also forbid the pagan double standard of allowing married men to have extramarital sex and mistresses. In all these ways, Christ-following women enjoyed far greater security and equality than women in the surrounding culture did.[25]

Someone once asked Mother Teresa what she saw as she walked the streets of Kolkata where the poorest of the poor lived and what she saw when she looked at the orphans, the starving, and the dying. "I see Jesus in a distressing disguise,"[26] she said. Few would argue against the impact Mother Teresa had in India and around the world. Mother Teresa's impact came directly from her view of the value of people made in God's image.

After observing that the Civil Rights movement was essentially a "Christian religious revival," Keller notes that when Martin Luther King, Jr. confronted racism in the white Church of the South, he did not call on Southern churches to become more secular.[27] Dr. King's sermons and his "Letter from a Birmingham Jail" invoked God's moral law and the Scripture. He called white Christ followers to be true to their own beliefs. He did not say, "Truth is relative, and everyone is free to decide what is right or wrong for them." If everything is relative, there would have been no incentive for white people in the South to give up their power. Rather, Dr. King invoked the prophet Amos, who said, "Let justice roll down like waters and righteousness as a mighty stream" (Amos 5:24). Dr. King knew that the antidote to racism was not less biblical influence, but more.[28]

When Martin Luther King, Jr. confronted racism in the white Church of the South, he did not call on Southern churches to become more secular ... Dr. King knew that the antidote to racism was not less biblical influence, but more.

Belief in the dignity of all humans has been the main force behind Christians protesting abortion. Though secularists often do not cite abortion as a cause of death, more Americans die each year through abortion than by any other cause. In 2018 over one million American babies were killed through abortion. Over 50 million babies were killed or aborted around the world. A high percentage of those aborted in the USA are African Americans and Hispanics. Whether born or unborn, human life of all ethnicities reflects the image of God and is worthy of protection instead of death.

Unborn children matter to God. The Psalmist says, "You formed my inward parts; you knitted me together in my mother's womb. I praise You for I am fearfully and wonderfully made" (Ps 139:13-14). The first person to recognize Jesus as Messiah was John the Baptist as he leapt while still in the womb of his mother, Elizabeth (Luke 1:41). Christ followers have historically rallied to protect the extremely vulnerable unborn, recognizing their value when others in culture do not.

Throughout history, the value God places on all those made in His image has immensely impacted the way Christ followers have treated others. Christians have lived from the worldview belief that people matter to God and should therefore matter to His followers. The value we place on people is a critical piece of our worldview and informs the way we respond to individuals and social dilemmas. A worldview that honors people also honors the God in whose image people are created.

More Americans die each year through abortion than by any other cause.

Christ followers have historically led in social justice because of their belief in the value of people and their embrace of the second greatest commandment, "you shall love your neighbor as yourself." Maintaining this heart for people is essential for a Christian worldview. People matter to God immensely and they should also matter to us.

How Do You See It?

1. While He was on earth, how did Jesus demonstrate the value of people?

2. Christians are *not* perfect, yet the biblical view of all people as image bearers of God has highly impacted the way Christians have treated others. Historically, what are some examples of Christians treating others with dignity, especially when such dignity was not common in their era?

3. Today, which humans struggle to receive dignity from secular postmodern culture?

CHAPTER THIRTEEN

HOW JESUS SAW HIMSELF

*"And a second is like it: You shall love
your neighbor as yourself."*
Matthew 22:39-40

Just as a Christian worldview affirms the value of *other* people, it also affirms the value of *oneself*. In God's eyes we are extremely valuable, and we need to see ourselves as He sees us: priceless. Just as others are valuable image bearers of God, *so are we*!

No one better modeled a healthy view of self than Jesus. He knew without a doubt that the Father had sent Him and loved Him immeasurably. John 13:3-5 gives us even more insight into Jesus' balancing humility with confidence:

Jesus, knowing that the Father had given all things into his hands, and that he had come from God and was going back to God, rose from supper. He laid aside his outer garments and taking a towel, tied it around his waist. Then He poured water into a basin and began to wash the disciples' feet and to wipe them with the towel that was wrapped around him.

As God, Jesus uniquely saw who He was. He saw His inheritance, that the Father had given all things into His hands (John 13:3b). Jesus also saw who He was—God who had come to earth. He knew that He had come from God (v. 3c), and He saw His future. He was going back to God (v. 3d). This strong sense of identity—knowing His inheritance, knowing where He had come from, and knowing where He was going—enabled Jesus to humble himself greatly by stripping off the clothing of honor and taking the position of a servant.

God also wants to give us such a strong sense of identity in Him that when God leads, we can serve anyone in any circumstance. Our identity does not come from the people we serve, where we serve, or even how we serve. Our identity comes from the One who made us in His image, loved us, and redeemed us!

Jesus further demonstrated that we do not need to prove our identity. At His baptism, God declared over Jesus, "You are my beloved Son, with You I am well pleased" (Matt 3:17; Mark 1:11). Then Jesus was led into the wilderness where the tempter began testing His identity, saying, "If you are the Son of God, command these stones to become loaves of bread" (Matt 4:3).

The enemy repeatedly left out one of the most important parts of Jesus' and our identity. The adjective "beloved" was not mentioned by the devil in his question to Jesus—perhaps because it was too painful to acknowledge, but more likely because the enemy did not want to reinforce such a powerful truth. Jesus was God's *beloved* Son. Jesus was greatly loved by His Father. We also are greatly loved by God our Father.

Our identity as loved by God gives us great strength in the midst of challenging circumstances. It reminds us that God cares for us and feels our pain with us. This identity is one that is *received*, not one that is achieved. We do not have to do anything to be firm in Christ's love. We can be confident that we are greatly beloved and that God is working on our behalf.

The adjective "beloved" was not mentioned by the devil in his question to Jesus—perhaps because it was too painful to acknowledge, but more likely because the enemy did not want to reinforce such a powerful truth.

Seeing himself as beloved in spite of the devil's omission, Jesus did not fall into the trap of proving His identity. He did not turn the stones to bread to demonstrate His Sonship. Jesus did not throw himself from the pinnacle of the temple to prove God's protection. Jesus also refused to worship the devil in exchange for the kingdoms of the world.

Jesus was God's beloved Son both because of who He ontologically was (His identity) and because of who God said He was. We also are children of God because as humans created in God's image, we have placed our faith in Christ. God has declared us His children. As John 1:12 says, "But to all who did receive him, who believed in his name, he gave the right to become children of God." We do not need to prove our identity in Christ. God said regarding Jesus, "This is my Beloved Son in whom I am well pleased" (Matt 3:17) *before* Jesus had done any miracles or public ministry. Jesus did not need to perform in order to be considered beloved of God, and neither do we. We cannot work any harder to become more loved by Him. We are significant because of God's love and His image already in our lives. God has made us that way.

How Do You See It?

1. How did Jesus demonstrate security in His identity?

2. Do you sometimes struggle with believing you are beloved of God? Why?

3. How does the way we see ourselves affect the way we serve others?

CHAPTER FOURTEEN

SEEING OUR OWN WORTH

"For we are God's masterpiece."
Ephesians 2:10a, NLT

On March 28, 1990, The Chicago Bulls defeated the Cleveland Cavaliers 117-113. Michael Jordan scored 69 of the points for the Bulls, the most points ever in his illustrious basketball career. Stacey King, a rookie forward with the Bulls added only one point from the foul line, but in an interview after the game, King made the following remark: "I will always remember the time Michael Jordan and I combined for 70 points."[1] Stacey King did not do much scoring that night, but he was still seemingly able to keep a reasonable amount of self-esteem in place. It wasn't about how well he performed. What mattered was who was on his team.

As followers of Christ, we also need to see our own worth, not based on our achievement or perceived worth by others around us, but as coming from God himself. We are valuable because we reflect His image. We are made in His likeness. We are also a part of His family, His team!

"I will always remember the time Michael Jordan and I combined for 70 points."
–Stacy King

Just as the enemy tries to devalue other humans, he tries to pervert our self-perception. We desperately need to have God's view of who we are! God's love and the intrinsic value of being made in His image must inform every thought and action we take. We need to live from the identity Christ gives us.

As we consider how we view ourselves, we need to be aware of two extremes of danger: pride and false humility. Thinking too highly or too lowly of ourselves is hazardous for fulfilling the potential God has put on our lives. Both views are incorrect, because at the center of each is a preoccupation with self.

One Extreme: Pride,
Seeing Ourselves as Important Apart from God

> "Pride is like bad breath. Everyone knows
> you have it except you."[2]

As believers we must always be wary of thinking too highly of ourselves, as the following story illustrates:

> A tall gentleman was anxiously standing in line at the airport check-in counter. Others who had also arrived late for the flight were in line ahead of him. They too became anxious as they watched the door to the jetway close. When the gentleman realized what was happening and that the gate agent was going to have to rebook some of the people in line, he jumped ahead of the line to take the matter into his own hands.

"Excuse me, Miss, but I need to get on this flight," he said.

She replied, "Yes, sir, and so do the rest of the people who are in line in front of you. Now kindly take your place back in line and we'll help you when it is your turn."

The tall gentleman didn't like being put off, and he thought being a little more forceful would help. So, he told her, "You see, if I don't get on that flight, I'm going to miss my meeting. And if you make me miss my meeting, I'm going to be very angry with you."

The agent calmly replied, "Sir, we'll help you when it's your turn."

Having had enough, the man, a vice president of a large company, glared at her and growled, "Do you know who I am?"

Also, having had enough, the agent picked up the microphone and announced, "Ladies and gentlemen, may I have your attention please. This gentleman at the desk does not seem to know who he is. If anyone can identify him, we would all greatly appreciate your assistance." The vice president returned to his place in line.[3]

Satan fell into the trap of self-importance. God created him beautifully, but Satan neglected to give God the credit He was due, and Satan was expelled from heaven. Today, the enemy tries to get us to follow his example. He wants our pride to push us away from God. In both good times and bad, we consistently need God to help us remember the source of the dignity we have. We are important because God made us in His image and has given us dignity in His Kingdom!

We are important because God made us in His image and has given us dignity in His Kingdom!

We have all met people whose heads are too big for their shoulders. As Franciscan Richard Rohr writes,

Humility and honesty are really the same thing. A humble

person is simply a brutally honest person about the whole truth. You and I came along a few years ago, and we're going to be gone in a few years. The only honest response to life is a humble one.[4]

Our goal should not be in being "big," but rather being humble with faith in a big God! To best see ourselves we must remember how big God is. As Warren Wiersbe said, "You can never be too small for God to use, only too big."[5]

Another Extreme: False Humility, Thinking Too Lowly of Ourselves

"Too humble is half-proud."[6]
—*Yiddish Proverb*

Another error in the way we see ourselves is with false humility or a poor self-image. Brennan Manning writes in *Ruthless Trust,*

A poor self-image reveals a lack of humility. Feelings of insecurity, inadequacy, inferiority, and self-hatred rivet our attention on ourselves. Humble men and women do not have a low opinion of themselves; they have no opinion of themselves, because they so rarely think about themselves. The heart of humility lies in undivided attention to God, a fascination with his beauty revealed in creation, a contemplative presence to each person who speaks to us, and a 'de-selfing' of our plans, projects, ambitions and soul. Humility is manifested in an indifference to our intellectual, emotional, and physical well-being and a carefree disregard of the image we present. No longer concerned with appearing to be good, we can move freely in the mystery of who we really are, aware of the sovereignty of God and of our absolute insufficiency and yet moved by a spirit of radical self-acceptance without self-concern.[7]

As the Rabbi of Kotzk said, "It took one day to get the Israelites out of Egypt. But it took forty years to get Egypt out of the Israelites."[8] For 400 years the Israelites had been slaves, and they continued to see themselves in that way for some time as they wandered through the desert. God had to work in the lives of the Israelites to help them see themselves as free, as being His people.

The most important conversations, briefings, meetings and lectures you will ever hear are those you hold in the privacy of your own mind.

As humans, we derive our dignity from God, as Helmut Thielicke says well: "His [humankind's] greatness rests solely on the fact that God in his incomprehensible goodness has bestowed his love upon him. God does not love us because we are so valuable; we are valuable because God loves us."[9] So, human dignity has two sides. As human beings we are dignified, but we are not to be proud of it, for our dignity is borne as a reflection of the Ultimately Dignified.

The most important conversations, briefings, meetings, and lectures you will ever hear are those you hold in the privacy of your own mind. Too often we engage in conversations that diminish the dignity God has given us and allow devaluing thoughts to have credibility in our minds.

At the exact moment a sperm penetrates an egg, the egg releases billions of zinc atoms that emit light. When our life started, sparks flew, literally! We are that amazing!

On a lighter note, embryologists have recently captured the moment of conception via fluorescence microscopy. What they discovered is that at the exact moment a sperm penetrates an egg, the egg releases billions of zinc atoms that emit light. When our life started, sparks flew, literally![10] We are that amazing (in God's eyes and under a microscope)!

Both seeing ourselves too highly with pride or too lowly with bad self-esteem are misperceptions of who we are in Christ. God alone knows how to dignify us without flattering and to humble us without humiliating. We need God's help to consistently live with a biblical worldview full of appropriate self-confidence and true dependence on Him.

How Do You See It?

1. How does knowing you are made in God's image impact your self-perception?

2. What are two extremes of inaccurate self-perception? With which extreme do you struggle the most?

3. Share your thoughts about Helmut Thielke's quote: "God does not love us because we are so valuable; we are valuable because God loves us."[11]

CHAPTER FIFTEEN

REFUSING LIES

"If we do not know what God thinks about us,
we will listen to what the enemy says about us."
—*Todd White*

S ometimes the devil omits part of our identity as he did with
Jesus during the temptation in the wilderness. Probably more
often, though, he uses lies to twist our self-understanding.
When we believe lies, we empower the liar. We need to be careful
not to give the enemy authority in our lives by believing his lies.

When we believe lies,
we empower the liar.

Here are some common lies of identity that can distort our
view of ourselves, and thus, our worldview:

1. **I am what I have.** Too often we allow our self-worth to be determined by the device we use, the clothes we wear, or the car we drive. As we get older, the house we own or our net worth may be part of this lie. In opposition, Jesus says, "One's life does not consist in the abundance of his possessions" (Luke 12:15).

2. **I am what I do.** We are not human doings. We are human *beings* created with inherent worth. God proclaimed that He was pleased with Jesus before Jesus had done any public ministry. Jesus did not have to "make it" or produce anything to be called significant by God, and neither do we!

3. **I am what other people say or think of me.** Other people do not have the right to define who you are. They did not create you. God did. He uniquely designed us and knows our purpose far better than anyone else, even ourselves. We should never allow others to dictate our identity.

4. **I am nothing more than my worst moment.** We have all made mistakes. We have all done things we regret and do not want to be remembered for doing. The good news is that God makes us new creations in Christ when we come to Him. Even if we do something wrong after coming to Christ, we can ask forgiveness. There is "no condemnation for those who are in Christ" (Rom 8:1). God can enable us to move beyond our mistakes with a fresh start.

5. **I am nothing less than my best moment.**[1] We should celebrate our successes, and give God credit for them, but those moments do not last forever. We should never build our identity only on our wins as others will later break our records or outperform our accomplishments.

6. **I am my sexual attractions.** God created sex, but He does not define us by our sexual appetites, whether good or bad. God defines us by what He has done for us and by our relationship with Him. Having a sexual attraction does

not define who we are, and it should not be our primary identification. Having an attraction alone is not sin. Acting on wrong sexual attractions is sin, and we need God's forgiveness and grace to overcome. No matter for whom or what someone has a sexual attraction, though, he or she should never be identified by that attraction.

7. **I am only my ethnicity.** Partial truths are dangerous. As a Christ follower, our first and primary identity comes from our relationship to the One who created us and is Lord of all. We are His sons and daughters and members of the body of Christ. Yes, we all have ethnicities which are a part of our identity. Our ethnic identity, though, is not our most important allegiance, and it is not what unites us with the body of Christ. Sure, we may celebrate our ethnicities, but we have to be careful as we do so. We must remember our common spiritual identity as members of Christ's family. The celebration of our ethnicity should never exclude other members of the Body of Christ.

Christ followers must remember who we are in Christ. Identity-amnesia will kill us. We must live from who we are and what God has done for us. Though our feelings may try to tell us we do not measure up, God can help us grasp the truth that we are His sons and daughters! (See Strategy #11.)

How we view ourselves and other people are strategically critical parts of our worldview. As Christians we must consider the second Greatest Commandment, "You shall love your neighbor as yourself" (Matt 22:38), as a foundation of how we see and treat others and ourselves. Jesus saw the value of people and gave His life for them. We should see people as Christ did and love them as He did.

How Do You See It?

1. With which of the seven identity lies listed in this chapter have you struggled most?

2. What other lie(s) have you sometimes believed?

3. What have you personally done to overcome lies?

PART FOUR:

Seeing The Great Commission Clearly

"Go therefore and make disciples of all nations, baptizing them in the name of the Father and of the Son and of the Holy Spirit, teaching them to observe all that I have commanded you."

Matthew 28:19-20

CHAPTER SIXTEEN

JESUS' LAST COMMAND: THE GREAT COMMISSION

"The Great Commission is not an option to be considered: it is a command to be obeyed."[1]
—Hudson Taylor

In His teachings and actions, Jesus clearly affirms the Old Testament commandments to love God and to love people. If we want to see well, we must love God and people, but there is another essential ingredient of clear vision. We must understand and prioritize the assignment Jesus gave us in His final command—the Great Commission.

Jesus was intentional in emphasizing our assignment. After His resurrection, Jesus spent forty days with His disciples and taught them many things (Acts 1:3), but we only have record of Jesus repeating *two* themes more than once. He repeated the importance of His resurrection (Mark 16:14; Luke 24:25-43; John 20:24-29), and He repeated the Church's assignment: the Great Commission. Each of the Gospels as well as Acts contains Jesus' last command to His disciples:

> And Jesus came and said to them, "All authority in heaven and on earth has been given to me. Go therefore and make disciples of all nations, baptizing them in the name of the Father and of the Son and of the Holy Spirit, teaching them to observe all that I have commanded you. And behold, I am with you always, to the end of the age" (Matt 28:18-20).

> And he said to them, "Go into all the world and proclaim the gospel to the whole creation. Whoever believes and is baptized will be saved, but whoever does not believe will be condemned. And these signs will accompany those who believe: in my name they will cast out demons; they will speak in new tongues; they will pick up serpents with their hands; and if they drink any deadly poison, it will not hurt them; they will lay their hands on the sick, and they will recover" (Mark 16:15-18).

> ... and said to them, "Thus it is written, that the Christ should suffer and on the third day rise from the dead, and that repentance for the forgiveness of sins should be proclaimed in his name to all nations, beginning from Jerusalem. You are witnesses of these things. And behold, I am sending the promise of my Father upon you. But stay in the city until you are clothed with power from on high" (Luke 24:46-49).

> Jesus said to them again, "Peace be with you. As the Father has sent me, even so I am sending you." And when he had said this, he breathed on them and said to them, "Receive the Holy Spirit. If you forgive the sins of any, they are forgiven them; if you withhold forgiveness from any, it is withheld" (John 20:21-23).

> He said to them . . . "But you will receive power when the Holy Spirit has come upon you, and you will be my witnesses in Jerusalem and in all Judea and Samaria, and to the ends of the earth" (Acts 1:7-8).

All Christ followers who wish to see clearly must see the Great Commission as their assignment. Jesus never qualified the assignment by indicating that some of His disciples would be exempt from involvement. He never said, "Some of you should love me with your whole, heart, mind, and strength," or "Some of you should love your neighbor as yourself." No, of course not! In the same way, no qualification is given to the Great Commission. Jesus asks and expects every believer to play a role in the Great Commission.

Every Believer Has a Local and a Global Role

Every believer having a role in the Great Commission does not mean that every believer has the *same* role in the Great Commission. Generally speaking, every believer has a local role and a role with the greater body of Christ, a global role. Locally, all believers should be discipling those in their spheres of influence within their culture of residence. Everyone's role will vary greatly as different parts of our culture need to be impacted in different ways, and we are each sent into different vocations that impact different parts of our culture. Our obedience to disciple those within our sphere of influence in our culture remains critical to seeing the Great Commission completed. Every part of the Body deserves honor for faithfully fulfilling the local role God assigns him or her.

Over 40 percent of the world still lives among people groups who have no access to the good news.

Every believer also has a global role in seeing the Great Commission completed where the Church does not yet exist. Yes, believers must locally participate in the Great Commission in their own sphere of influence, but we must also remember each version of the Great Commission emphasizes the immense importance of *all nations* having access to the gospel. Over two thousand years after Christ gave us the Great Commission, we are still miserably short of reaching the goal of discipling every ethnic group. Over 40 percent of the world still lives among people groups who have no access to the good news.[2] The importance of all nations, or *ethne* in Greek (Matt 28:19), having the opportunity to respond to the gospel cannot be overstated. Jesus paid the price for *all* nations, and He commissioned us to be a part of their discipleship.

Not every believer is called to go to those yet unreached with the Gospel, but worldwide less than one out of five thousand Christians serve as cross-cultural missionaries.[3] Of this small number of cross-cultural missionaries, less than ten percent serve the world's unreached.[4] This means, those most in need of cross-cultural missionaries are normally neglected.

Worldwide, less than one out of five thousand Christians serve as cross-cultural missionaries.

Far less than one percent of Christian giving goes to making disciples among unreached people groups. Americans spend more on Halloween costumes for their pets than they do on reaching the unreached with the gospel.[5] We can do better. We must do better.

If it is not Christ's desire for any to perish (1 Tim 2:4, 2 Pet 3:9), why are so few of His disciples engaging those without access to His truth? Why does way over 99 percent of Christian giving go to areas of the world and people groups who already have an existing church?

Not every believer is called to cross cultures, learn new languages, and follow the calling of a full-time missionary, but every believer does have a global role in reaching unreached people groups around the world. Everyone can pray for people groups still unreached with the good news and for the missionaries serving among them. Every believer can also give financially on a regular basis. Some believers may also be able to serve on short-term cross-cultural trips, assisting long-term missionaries in seeing the unreached discipled for Christ. There are many ways to assist long-term workers in planting the church among the unreached. These include helping with business platforms, assistance with children's education, prayer support, regular encouragement, and meeting other miscellaneous felt needs.

Christ emphasizes His longing for all nations to have access to the gospel by repeating this desire in Scripture five times. Each version of the Great Commission includes a unique emphasis, something Jesus wanted to highlight. The next section briefly examines these unique aspects. Each repetition provides more insight into how believers are to see the Great Commission completed in every nation.

How Do You See It?

1. After His resurrection, what two themes did Jesus repeat?
2. How does every believer have both a local and a global role in the Great Commission? What are your roles?
3. After 2,000 years, why do you think over 40 percent of the world are still part of people groups unreached with the gospel?

CHAPTER SEVENTEEN

DISCIPLESHIP: THE UNIQUENESS OF MATTHEW'S VERSION

*And Jesus came and said to them,
"All authority in heaven and on earth has
been given to me. Go therefore and make
disciples of all nations, baptizing them in the
name of the Father and of the Son and of the Holy
Spirit, teaching them to observe all that I have
commanded you. And behold, I am with
you always, to the end of the age."*
Matthew 28:18-20

Matthew 28:18-20 is perhaps the most famous version of the Great Commission. Many unique features stand out, including Jesus' *authority* to give the Great Commission and the *promise of His presence* with us as we work with Him to complete our assignment. Perhaps most striking, however, is Jesus' emphasis on *discipleship*.

Jack Canfield and Mark Hansen share a story about a teacher giving a lesson on Jesus and His disciples to a kindergarten class. The teacher was feeling quite proud of his lesson. It was a model lesson, an A+. The teacher felt he hit a homerun!

At the conclusion of the lesson, the teacher opened the discussion to questions. The students wildly waved their arms. The lesson was obviously a success. Teaching seemed so rewarding. It would be exciting to hear all the children had learned from such a great lesson.

Brittney's arm was waving more frantically than the rest—surely her observation would be that much more brilliant, thought the teacher. "Brittney, what do you have to say about Jesus and His disciples?" the teacher asked eagerly.

"Well," she began, with true kindergarten confidence, "I just wanted you to know that I know a lot about disciples 'cause at my house we disciple everything. We have a special disciple can for plastic, a special disciple can for glass, and a special disciple can for paper. My mom says it's how we save the earth."

The teacher paused, took a deep breath, and said, "Let's get ready for snack time."[1]

Unfortunately, our culture has lost the true meaning of "disciple" and the importance of discipleship as we follow Christ.

Jesus prioritized discipleship. "Going" is the first participle in Matthew's Great Commission, and the verb, "Go" is very important to Great Commission obedience, as are baptizing and teaching. Missionaries must go to bring the gospel to people groups who have no church. The main verb in Matthew 28:19, though, is "Make disciples" or "disciple." We make disciples by going, baptizing, and teaching. Making Christ's discipleship available to all nations is the heart of the Great Commission.

Jesus modeled discipleship in His ministry on earth. Mark 3 shares how Jesus called and equipped His disciples:

> And he went up on the mountain and called to him those whom he desired, and they came to him. And he appointed twelve (whom he also named apostles) so that they might be with him and he might send them out to preach and have authority to cast out demons (Mark 3:13-15).

A key way Jesus discipled His disciples was by spending time with them and giving them opportunities to do what He did (preaching and casting out demons).

The most common Greek word for "disciple" is *mathetes*. It is often translated as "disciple," but it can also be translated as "learner." A *mathetes* of Jesus is one who learns from Him. Learning ideally should happen in a variety of environments, including mentorship, teaching, and on the job training.

Baptism:
Public Confession of Discipleship

Baptism is a key part of discipleship. In Christ's day, Gentiles turning to Judaism were baptized in water as part of their conversion process. Baptism was commonly recognized as a religious rite. Jesus' cousin and prophetic forerunner was even known as "John the Baptist." John baptized Jews as they repented for forgiveness of sins.[2] Jesus instructed His followers to make disciples of all nations and to baptize them in the name of the Father, Son and Holy Spirit.

There is an apocryphal story in which a boy talks with his pastor about his new faith in Christ. At one point the boy asks the pastor, "When do I take the next step? I mean, when am I going to be advertised?"

The boy meant to say "baptized," but inadvertently switched the words. Yet, his misspeak emphasizes the role that water baptism plays in our lives as Christians. Baptism advertises our new allegiance to Christ and our new identity in Him.

Baptism is a part of discipleship that helps new believers see themselves as part of Christ's Body. In Galatians, Paul emphasizes, "For in Christ Jesus you are all sons of God, through faith. For as many of you as were baptized into Christ have put on Christ. There is neither Jew nor Greek, there is neither slave nor free, there is no male and female, for you are all one in Christ Jesus" (3:26-28).

In Buddhist, Hindu, and Muslim contexts, water baptism is especially seen as a major statement of community belonging. Many Buddhist, Hindu and Muslim families see baptism as much more than a profession of faith in Christ, but as a ceremony that moves them from their former community into the Christian community.

No matter what one's community is before coming to Christ, one's primary identity after following Jesus is in Jesus himself and His Body.

Baptism's role in discipleship is a public statement of an inner faith in Christ and membership in His Body. No matter what one's community is before coming to Christ, one's primary identity after following Jesus is in Jesus himself and His Body. One's birth identity may have been a Hindu caste, but after faith in Christ, the new believer's identity is now in Christ and His Body. Before Christ, one may have been a Muslim, but after Christ, one's identity is in the ONE who gave His life for us. Baptism symbolizes this change of identity from being dead without Christ to being alive with Him.

Obedience:
The Content and Goal of Discipleship

"... teaching these new disciples to obey
all the commands I have given you ... "
Matthew 28:20a, NLT

Countless curricula have been written to disciple believers. Most of these curricula focus on content to be taught and memorized. Scope and sequences are not bad. Objectives are not wrong *per se*, but an emphasis away from what Jesus prescribed can easily lead to majoring in the minors.

In Matthew 28:20, what Jesus asked believers to teach new disciples is both simple and profoundly difficult: *obedience!* Jesus commanded us to teach disciples *to obey* all the commands He had given them. Jesus never said, "Teach new disciples everything I taught you," or "Teach the new disciples all the commands I gave you." Instead, He commanded us to teach the new disciples *to obey*. Teaching obedience is not complicated, but it can be hard to model. May God help us live lives totally surrendered to Him! May we live like Jesus who learned obedience through the things He suffered (Heb 5:8). We also learn obedience by submitting our lives to God and being willing to suffer if necessary to follow through with His commands. Jesus is calling us to teach disciples to live lives fully surrendered to Him.

107

Discipling All Nations

The Greek phrase, μαθητεύσατε πάντα τὰ ἔθνη, in Matthew 28:19 is often translated "make disciples of all nations." This translation encourages us to make individual disciples in all nations, and particularly makes sense in individualistic cultures. We should never diminish the great importance of seeing individuals discipled in obeying Christ.

A more literal way to translate μαθητεύσατε πάντα τὰ ἔθνη though is "discipling all nations." This translation emphasizes the importance of impacting the cultures of nations. As missionaries focus on making disciples and planting churches, the believers from those churches should then be salt and light in their cultures. The Church should impact the values and behavior within nations and seek to see nations' cultures transformed to reflect God's values and heart. Some modern writers have even referred to "discipling nations" as creating culture.[3]

Jesus wants all ethnicities on earth to reflect the values of heaven. He even challenges us to pray for His Kingdom to come and His will to be done on earth as it is in heaven (Matt 6:10). All cultures on earth have been marred by the effects of sin (Rom 3:23), but God wants to bring redemption through His people.

In 1975 God independently gave both Bill Bright, founder of Campus Crusade for Christ, and Loren Cunningham, founder of Youth with a Mission, a vision for the reaching of seven different spheres of influence or mountains in culture.[4] A day before they met each other, God gave the same vision to both men. When they met the next day, they were astounded at the similarity of revelation they had both received. About a month later God gave Francis Schaeffer the same concept.[5] The seven spheres of influence God showed Bill, Loren, and Francis are as follows:

- Family
- The Church

- Education
- Business, Science and Technology
- Government and Politics
- Arts, Entertainment, and Sports
- Media

Cunningham later learned that 100 years before, in 1875, Abraham Kuyper had written about a similar concept, called "sphere sovereignty."[6] As Kuyper studied John Calvin's writings, he learned God is not to be categorized into a religious box, affecting only religion. God was to be Lord of all areas of life, though the Church was not to seek a theocracy or to rule over the other spheres directly. Kuyper only delineated five spheres in his model, but the concept was remarkably similar.[7]

The *family* is considered the foundational sphere of the seven, and parents, by nature of their role, disciple their children. God wants this discipleship to honor Him and to point children toward His truth. Discipling one's children in Christ is a parent's greatest ministry.

God also wants the *Church* to disciple believers and to equip them for impacting other spheres of their nation. Apostles, prophets, evangelists, pastors and teachers are to equip God's people for ministry (not just in church environments) and for building up the body of Christ (Eph 4:11-12).

Believers engaged in a nation's *education* also have a critical role. Contrary to popular secular thought, education is never value-neutral. Educators promote worldviews. From daycares to universities, Christian educators have the opportunity to disciple nations from a worldview that honors God.

Businesses operating with God's values add much value to nations. Jobs, income, services for all peoples, development, tax revenues, opportunities for advancement, and a thriving economy all result when business is done well in a nation. One of the most effective tools for overcoming poverty in any nation is business done with biblical values. Countries all around the world have benefited from the economic uplift of businesses.

God cares about a nation's *politics* and uses His disciples as salt and light in systems that often need redemption. Christ's disciples in politics should govern with heaven's values, aligning themselves first with Christ's causes, not with a particular party's platform. A nation's people are blessed when godly politicians serve the nation with integrity.

God also wants those in the arenas of *arts*, *entertainment*, and *sports* to express the values of heaven. God's creativity and excellence should shine forth from the lives of believers who serve in this important part of culture. May believers engaged in arts and sports use the platforms God gives them to glorify Him and acknowledge Him.

Believers called to the sphere of *media* are also called to serve by communicating their message in ways that honor God, people, and truth. One of Jesus' names is the Word, and God is the supreme communicator. With advances in technology and the speed with which messages are sent, more than ever nations need communication that honors truth and God's values.

Warning!

The goal of discipling and influencing the seven mountains or spheres of influence is not to "take over" these areas or to exert political power in them (dominion theology), but rather to allow God's will for these spheres to be manifest on earth as it is in heaven. We also must be careful with spiritual warfare language that can be easily misunderstood as offensive by non-believers.

Believers do not have to be top leaders in these mountains to actively disciple others within these mountains in Christ's values and desires. Christ did not commission us to control or win, but to disciple to obedience (Matt 28:19). As Nancy Pearcey shares, "We can make a significant difference within our sphere of influence—but only as we 'crucify' our craving for success, power, and public acclaim."[8] In Jesus' words, "If anyone would come after me, let him deny himself and take up his cross daily and follow me" (Luke 9:23). Whatever influence God gives in any sphere must be used for His glory and for the benefit of His Kingdom, not for personal gain.

How Do You See It?

1. Part of discipleship is baptism, a demonstration of the new life we have in Christ. Have you been baptized? Are you encouraging others to be baptized?

2. In Matthew's version of the Great Commission, Jesus emphasized obedience to His commands as the main content of teaching. How are you teaching obedience? Is there an area of your life where God is asking you to obey Him more?

3. God is concerned about every nation (people group) and every part of every nation. To what nation is God calling you, and what part(s) of that nation is He calling you to disciple for Him?

CHAPTER EIGHTEEN

PROCLAMATION: THE UNIQUENESS OF MARK'S VERSION

*"Go into all the world and proclaim
the gospel to the whole creation."*
Mark 16:15

Mark's version of the Great Commission emphasizes proclamation. As Christ followers we must prioritize the proclamation of the good news of Jesus Christ. We must see ourselves as proclaimers of truth.

Proclaiming is not always popular in Western society. The enemy uses fear to keep the Church silent; he does not want the truth of the gospel to be shared with anyone. To break this silence, Dick Brogden urges us to open our mouths and proclaim:

> The forces of your age seek to muzzle you. The siren song of respectability urges moderation. Powers within, powers without, and powers from below make it their one ambition to silence the compelling, consistent verbalized presentation of the gospel. You are pressured not to offend. You are persuaded not to inflame. You are badgered towards suffocating tolerance. Impress on your thinking anew, Jesus' words brought division. He came to bring not peace, but a sword. The words of John the Baptist brought his beheading. Stephen's steady sermons summoned stones down on his head. Yes, in the kingdom we attack injustice wherever we find it, but you want a justice issue? Let us not waver from the greatest of them all! Not all are poor, not all are trafficked, not all are illiterate, not all lack clean water, and not all have AIDS, but all have sinned and fallen short of the glory of God (Rom. 3:23). Sin is the universal malady. You want a justice issue? Men and women, boys and girls, young and old, rich and poor, they perish. They die eternally. They suffer. They march in their legions towards damnable hell, not because of the excesses or hypocrisy of our fathers, but because of our thundering silence![1]

The gospel is good news. Let's not keep it to ourselves. Let us proclaim the birth, sinless life, death, and resurrection of Jesus. Let us proclaim salvation to all. May we share with others the hope we have in Christ and the love He has for all nations.

Proclaiming the gospel is a unique function of Christ's Body. No other part of our society is going to share how to be reconciled to God. Governments may provide education. Corporations may provide job training. Non-profits may do many good things like provide water, food, or clothing. Many organizations today emphasize the need to stop social evils like racism and trafficking. As believers we may partner with these groups to do good and serve our communities and nations. *Only Christ's disciples*, however, have the responsibility of proclaiming Christ.

For many years David Leatherberry served the poor in Afghanistan via food and milk distribution. He saw the importance of the Afghans receiving physical food, but he also recognized their desperate need for true spiritual food. He writes:

> If I lift the Afghan out of his poverty and do not proclaim Christ by my life and words, I do not love him. If in reality my first concern is relieving his physical suffering and not the eternal destiny of his soul, I do not love him. If I am only the hands and feet of Jesus and not his mouth also, I pervert the gospel and fail Christ.[2]

We want to be the hands and feet of Jesus, but we must never forget our essential role as *His mouth*. We must see ourselves as proclaimers of hope in a world that desperately needs the gospel.

Many organizations today emphasize the need to stop social evils like racism and trafficking. As believers we may partner with these groups ... Only Christ's disciples, however, have the responsibility of proclaiming Christ.

Not all proclamation is the same. Proclaiming Christ looks different in different contexts and in different parts of the world. Our own different personalities feel more comfortable with certain styles of proclamation than others. Whatever our style or personality, though, we as Christ followers must do the work of an evangelist (2 Tim 4:5). No matter if we are extroverted or introverted, quiet or loud, articulate or stammering, we must proclaim.

Raymond Nonnatus was a thirteenth-century Spanish missionary to Muslims who saw himself as a proclaimer. He went to Valencia where he ransomed 140 Christians from slavery. He then traveled to North Africa where he ransomed another 250 captives in Algiers. Nonnatus then went to Tunis where it is said he surrendered himself as a hostage to free twenty-eight captive Christians. Nonnatus suffered greatly in captivity. Legend states that the Muslims, concerned about his proclamation, bored a hole through his lips with a hot iron and padlocked his mouth to prevent him from preaching.[3] May we exhibit the bravery and tenacity of Nonnatus in proclamation!

Another unique element to Mark's version of the Great Commission is the promise Jesus gives of signs accompanying our proclamation of the gospel. These signs indicate God's concern for physical needs like deliverance from demons and healing from sickness. They also indicate God's desire to protect and help His disciples as they travel and proclaim the gospel. Most importantly, all these "signs" also point to Jesus and the truth of the message we proclaim. When the lame walk, people take note and are usually ready to listen to what the healer has to say. When someone does not die after being bitten by a poisonous snake, people pay attention. The signs would add weight to the disciples' words of proclamation.

We must see ourselves as proclaimers, as people called to be the light of the world. We must not remain silent. We must use words to make Christ known. We proclaim Christ with our actions, yes, but we must also proclaim Him with our words.

How Do You See It?

1. When was the last time you proclaimed Christ outside of a Christian environment?

2. Do you sometimes feel hesitant to proclaim Christ? Why? What does God want you to do to grow in proclamation?

3. All have sinned and fall short of God's glory (Rom 3:23). All need the gospel for hope and salvation. The unreached live among people groups that have very few if any Christians living among them that can proclaim the gospel to them. What are you doing to help the gospel be proclaimed to the unreached around the world?

CHAPTER NINETEEN

POWER: THE UNIQUENESS OF LUKE'S VERSION

And said to them, "Thus it is written, that the Christ should suffer and on the third day rise from the dead, and that repentance for the forgiveness of sins should be proclaimed in his name to all nations, beginning from Jerusalem. You are witnesses of these things. And behold, I am sending the promise of my Father upon you. But stay in the city until you are clothed with power from on high."
Luke 24:46-49

L uke's version of the Great Commission also mentions proclamation, but he emphasizes the role of the Holy Spirit in giving us power to fulfill our assignment. In the last part of Luke's version, Jesus pledges to send the promise of His Father upon His disciples (Luke 24:49b). Jesus then urges them, "But stay in the city until you are clothed with power from on high" (v. 49c).

Throughout His Gospel, Luke wants his readers to see the importance of the Holy Spirit. The Holy Spirit would fill John the Baptist before he was born (1:15). The Holy Spirit would divinely cause Mary (a virgin until after Christ was born) to get pregnant (v. 35). The Holy Spirit would inspire prophecy by Zechariah (v. 67), reveal Christ to Simeon (2:25-27), and descend upon Jesus in the form of a dove (3:22).

Luke emphasizes that Jesus was led by the Spirit into the wilderness (4:1) and returned in the power of the Spirit to Galilee (v. 14), where He read from Isaiah in the synagogue:

The Spirit of the Lord is upon me, because he has anointed me to proclaim good news to the poor. He has sent me to proclaim liberty to the captives and recovering of sight to the blind, to set at liberty those who are oppressed (4:18, italics added).

Luke continues in chapters 10 to 12 to help us see the importance of the Holy Spirit. Jesus rejoices in the Holy Spirit that His Father had revealed so much to His followers (10:21). He shares that His Father will give the Holy Spirit to those who ask Him (11:13). He warns against blasphemy against the Holy Spirit (12:10) and then immediately encourages His followers that the

Holy Spirit will teach them what they should say when they are persecuted or questioned (12:12).

Jesus modeled a life of dependence on the Holy Spirit and emphasized the need for His disciples to be Holy Spirit-empowered. Luke 23 records the extreme suffering Jesus endured in order for all humanity to be reconciled to God. His words in Luke 24 convey His deep desire for all nations (all *ethne)* to have repentance and forgiveness of sin proclaimed to them (24:47). Yet, there was something Jesus wanted more than His disciples' immediate obedience of the Great Commission: Jesus wanted them to be empowered![1]

Jesus wanted His disciples to be empowered for at least two reasons. First, *He knew that He was sending His disciples to do something impossible in their own strength.* He knew there was no way they could ever overcome spiritually without the empowerment of the Holy Spirit. Jesus knew that they needed to be endued with power from on high (24:49)!

Jesus also wanted the disciples to be empowered because He knew that unempowered disciples reproduce unempowered disciples.

Jesus also wanted the disciples to be empowered because *He knew that unempowered disciples reproduce unempowered disciples*[2] (if they reproduce at all). Each reproduces after its own kind. Jesus did not want us to reproduce weak followers of Christ, but disciples fully empowered by the Holy Spirit. Jesus wants us filled with the Spirit's power so our disciples will also tap into the Spirit's power and be able to stand firm in the midst of suffering and stand with power for the working of miracles.

Those serving among Muslims often share about three types of encounters Muslims typically need to experience before they acknowledge Christ: a love encounter, a truth encounter, and a power encounter. Muslims as well as most Buddhists and Hindus must encounter the power of God as part of their faith journey to Christ. Love encounters and truth encounters are necessary, but for the gospel to be received, a power encounter is normally required. Power encounters cannot happen without the Holy Spirit!

We must walk in the power of God so we can represent Christ well to others. As Paul writes to the Corinthians,

> And I, when I came to you, brothers, did not come proclaiming to you the testimony of God with lofty speech or wisdom. For I decided to know nothing among you except Jesus Christ and him crucified. And I was with you in weakness and in fear and much trembling, and my speech and my message were not in plausible words of wisdom, but in demonstration of the Spirit and of power, so that your faith might not rest in the wisdom of men but in the power of God (1 Cor 2:1-5).

Paul experienced the power of God on the road to Damascus and subsequently when Ananias prayed for his healing (Acts 9:1-17). Paul spoke in tongues more than all the Corinthians (1 Cor 14:18). He knew firsthand the great importance of Jesus' words, "But stay in the city until you are clothed with power from on high" (Luke 24:49c). It was this power that enabled Paul to plant churches throughout Asia Minor, to see people healed of all kinds of diseases, and to stand firm despite fierce persecution that would ultimately end his life. We also must see the great importance of being filled with the Holy Spirit as we fulfill the Great Commission

How Do You See It?

1. How does Luke emphasize the Holy Spirit in his Gospel?

2. Jesus came to earth to sacrifice His life and to prepare His disciples for the Great Commission. Yet, what did Jesus want even more than immediate obedience to the Great Commission? Why?

3. How did the Holy Spirit baptism change the disciples? Which change would you like to see in your own life?

CHAPTER TWENTY

BEING SENT: THE UNIQUENESS OF JOHN'S VERSION

Jesus said to them again, "Peace be with you. As the Father has sent me, even so I am *sending* you." And when he had said this, he breathed on them and said to them, "Receive the Holy Spirit. If you forgive the sins of any, they are forgiven them; if you withhold forgiveness from any, it is withheld."

John 20:21-23, italics added

John's Gospel emphasizes our role as sent ones in God's Kingdom. Just as the Father sent Jesus, so Jesus is sending us. Jesus did not come to simply live in the world, to simply breathe the air and reside with people. He recognized and knew He was sent to Earth with a purpose.

As believers, we also are sent into the world to represent Christ and to bring the forgiveness for which Christ gave His life. Jesus has placed us, indeed, sent us to our particular families, jobs, communities, and country. We are sent to bring Jesus into these places and relationships. We are not meant to just exist.

Jesus could have been disobedient to His Father. He could have forgotten the purpose for which He came to earth. We can do that as well, if we are not careful. When we choose not to proclaim the gospel or selectively decide certain people are not worth telling, we are disobeying God. Furthermore, we are withholding God's forgiveness and salvation from people who need that gift more than they need anything else on earth.

As sent ones, we can rest in the security of His authority. The One who overcame death has commissioned us to impact our assigned spheres of influence. He has commissioned us to bring His forgiveness and reconciliation. We are ambassadors for Christ, imploring others to be reconciled to God (2 Cor 5:20), and we go with His authority.

Will we see ourselves as ambassadors sent by God to our jobs, our schools, our neighborhoods, and our families? Will we live with the awareness that we represent not ourselves but the *One* who sent us? Will we represent His love and His values well?

The meaning of John 20:23 has been debated: "If you forgive the sins of any, they are forgiven them; if you withhold forgiveness from any, it is withheld." We understand that ultimately only God can forgive sin, and yet Jesus seems to be saying we as His disciples can have a part in forgiveness. One way to think about Christ followers forgiving sin is to think about their sharing the good news of forgiveness with others.

When believers proclaim the availability of Christ's forgiveness and invite people to receive it, we are in one sense playing a role in seeing people forgiven. If we refuse to proclaim Christ's forgiveness, we are in one sense refusing to let the sins of others be forgiven. Our role in proclamation is critical.

Will we live with the awareness that we represent not ourselves but the One who sent us?

As we are sent, will we let others know about the forgiveness Christ offers? Will we let them know that no matter what they have done, Christ's death is enough to pay the price? Will we share about the scars in his hands and side (20:20) and the price Jesus paid so we could be restored to Him? Or will we withhold the forgiveness *He* has so lavishly given us?

How Do You See It?

1. Do you see yourself as being sent by God to your family? school? job/business? neighborhood? What might that look like for you?

2. The people in your neighborhood and workspace need the forgiveness of Christ. What steps do you think God wants you to take so they can experience Christ?

3. God calls some to be sent outside their culture, so that those without access may respond to Christ's forgiveness. Are you open to God nudging you to go to a people group outside your own? Honestly share your hopes and fears with the Lord.

4. Think of those you know who have said, "Here am I; send me to those who do not know how to experience Christ's forgiveness." What can you do to encourage these sent ones?

CHAPTER TWENTY ONE

BOTH HERE AND ABROAD: THE UNIQUENESS OF ACTS' VERSION

"So when they had come together, they asked him, 'Lord, will you at this time restore the kingdom to Israel?' He said to them, 'It is not for you to know times or seasons that the Father has fixed by his own authority. But you will receive power when the Holy Spirit has come upon you, and you will be my witnesses in Jerusalem and in all Judea and Samaria, and to the ends of the earth.'"

Acts 1:6-8

A cts contains the last version of Christ's commission to the Church to spread the gospel all over this world. As a history of the Early Church, the book of Acts not only states the mission of the Church but then also narrates through 28 chapters how the Church followed Christ's command recorded in chapter 1.

The Acts version of the Great Commission emphasizes the both/ and nature of the Great Commission, that the mission of the Church is not just local, but also global. After emphasizing the need for the power of the Holy Spirit (which is also emphasized in the Gospel of Luke), Jesus shares geographical locations where His disciples would be his witnesses. These locations—Jerusalem, Judea, Samaria, and the ends of the earth—help us see the the scope of ministry Jesus intended for His followers.

The disciples were in Jerusalem when they received the Great Commission, but Jerusalem was not where they or their families were from. Most of the disciples were from Galilee (Judas Iscariot was the one exception; he was from west of the Dead Sea). The culture of Galilee would have differed greatly from the culture of Judea. Yet, Jesus commanded them to remain there until they had received the Holy Spirit. Then they were to start as His witnesses right where they were.

We also must view the Great Commission as starting where we are. God may lead us to other places, but we must be faithful in our present context. God has ministry and growth opportunities right where we are, and we are wise to partner with Him in these. Sometimes people are afraid to proclaim in their local context and yet sign up for a short-term trip to proclaim Christ in a foreign country. The problem is there is no magic in an airplane. We are the same person elsewhere as we are in our current location. We must obey Christ's command and proclaim His salvation where we live first.

Judea was the region surrounding Jerusalem. In Acts 1:8, Judea represents ministry in a near cultural environment. The setting will be outside our neighborhood or in a different city, but we will still proclaim Christ among people we are used to engaging.

Samaria was an area near Judea but separate in culture. It had been the capital of the Northern Kingdom of Israel, and much idolatry had taken place there. Samaritans were looked down upon by many Jews, yet they too needed to hear the gospel. Jesus had earlier demonstrated His concern for the people in this area when He travelled through Samaria on one of His journeys and ministered to the people of Sychar (John 4). Now Jesus underscores that He still is concerned that Samaritans have access to His good news. In Acts Jesus commissions witnesses to proclaim His message not only where they lived and in nearby areas, but also where they would need to cross cultural boundaries.

Jesus did not say, "Pick one of the following: Jerusalem, Judea, Samaria or the ends of the earth. That is your group. Proclaim there." No, Jesus used the word "and," emphasizing all of the locations.

Finally, "the ends of the earth" represents all the people groups of the earth that were not already covered by the first three groups. "End" would imply a finish line—a place far away, yet important in God's eyes. Matthew 28:19, Mark 16:15, and Luke 24:47 all indicate the great importance of making disciples and proclaiming the gospel to the ends of the earth. We are to keep proclaiming Jesus until *all* nations have heard the message.

Again, the Great Commission in Acts emphasizes a both/and approach. Jesus did not say, "Pick one of the following: Jerusalem, Judea, Samaria or the ends of the earth. That is your group. Proclaim there." No, Jesus used the word "and," emphasizing *all* of the locations. In other words, no believer is exempt from being a part of seeing their Jerusalem, Judea, Samaria and the ends of the earth reached. Churches must disciple their neighborhoods, maybe even their cities or regions, but they must also recognize their role in discipling every nation for the Kingdom. Jesus did not die only for the people who look like us or only for those who live near us. Neither does He commission the disciples to abandon Jerusalem and head to the ends of the earth. We are called to do both.

Seeing the Nations in Heaven

Revelation 7 shares a picture of what heaven will be like one day. People from every tongue, tribe, and people group will be gathered around God's throne worshipping Him. No people group will be left out. Representatives from every nation will give Him glory and honor. Will we be a part of seeing that happen? Will we pray? Will we give? Will we go to the jobs, neighborhoods, cities, states, countries and people groups to which God commissions us? Will we recognize our role in God's plan of redemption?

How Do You See It?

1. In what local ministries are you personally engaged?

2. What are you doing globally to be a part of making disciples where there is no church? Which missionaries do you support? Which missionaries do you regularly lift up in prayer?

3. Which version of the Great Commission stirs your heart the most? Why?

4. Did one of the versions of the Great Commission make you say, "Ouch!" What is God leading you to do?

PART FIVE:

Strategies for Seeing the Whole Elephant

It was our first train ride in India and one we would never forget. We were heading to a conference in South India, and we had the privilege of traveling with our first mentors in India, the Satyavratas. Our train departed from Bangalore in the evening, and we were to sleep overnight on individual, assigned berths before arriving the next morning in Cochin, Kerala.

The journey went well until the middle of the night when I needed to make a trip to the toilet. I rose, put on my shoes, and sauntered out of the dark compartment to a lit-up area between the train cars where the toilets were located.

When I returned to our compartment, I became confused in the dark. When I reached my bed, someone was sleeping there. Realizing I was in the wrong place, I quickly backed away. Then I checked the next compartment area, but the beds were full there also. So, I peeked in another couple of areas, desperately trying to find my berth.

By this time my eyes had begun to adjust better to the darkness of the compartment, and I somehow managed to check again in the first place I had looked. To my amazement I saw the most beautiful woman in the world lying on my bed! My newly adjusted eyes helped me recognize my wife, who had slipped down from her upper bunk to my lower berth, so she could better guard my laptop, which I had left on my bed when I went to the restroom. (We had been warned many times about thievery on the trains, specifically of laptops.)

Just as my eyes had to adjust to the darkness inside the train car so that I could recognize my wife, our spiritual eyes also must adjust, so that we perceive reality from God's perspective. We cannot see the whole elephant on our own, but with God's help we can see much better. The next fifteen chapters give fifteen different strategies for clearer spiritual perception. These are habits we can develop to help us perceive reality the way God does!

STRATEGY #1

START WITH GOD IN PRAYER

*"I have been driven many times to my knees
by the overwhelming conviction that I had
nowhere else to go."*
President Abraham Lincoln[1]

Turning to God for help is the first step in the journey to seeing as God sees. Since you are reading this book, you most likely have given your heart to Christ. If you have not surrendered to Christ, may I encourage you to do so—it will be the best decision you have ever made! God, our Creator, wants to help us see reality the way He does, and the first step is submitting to His Lordship. As we submit our lives to Christ, God gives us new life in Him.

Surrendering our life to God or being born again opens the door for greater spiritual insight. Jesus said in John 3:3, "Unless one is born from above, he cannot see the kingdom of God." This does not mean that non-believers cannot see anything or cannot be correct about many things, but rather, this verse indicates that part of reality cannot be perceived without God. As the Apostle Paul writes, "The natural person [a person who has not been born again] does not accept the things of the Spirit of God, for they are foolishness to him, and he is not able to understand them because they are spiritually discerned" (1 Cor 2:14). The devil has blinded many from seeing truth (2 Cor 4:4). When we profess Christ as our Lord, God works in our lives and gives us a new spiritual ability to see things that we could not see without God's help. At least some degree of spiritual blindness is removed by simply giving one's life to Christ.

Part of the reason this spiritual blindness is removed is because after surrendering our lives to Christ we become new creations in Christ. Paul writes in 2 Corinthians 5:17 that if anyone is in Christ, he or she is a new creation. Old things have passed away. All things have become new. Part of being a new creation is receiving a new set of spiritual eyes!

When blind Bartimaeus stood by Jericho on the roadside, he acknowledged his blindness and his need of healing. As he repeatedly cried out, "Jesus, Son of David, have mercy on me" (Mark 10:47), many rebuked him and told him to be silent. Even with all the cultural pressure to keep quiet, Bartimaeus cried out even more, "Son of David, have mercy on me" (v. 48). When Jesus asked him, "What do you want me to do for you?" Bartimaeus did not hesitate, "Rabbi, let me recover my sight" (v. 51). Bartimaeus had no difficulty admitting his need of sight to Jesus. He was desperate for Jesus' help. Jesus did not disappoint Bartimaeus, but rather commended him for his faith and healed him of his physical blindness (v. 52).

We, like Bartimaeus, need to recognize our need for sight. We need to continually seek God's assistance to see well spiritually. All spiritual blindness is not removed by giving our lives to Christ, but it is a critical first step! When we give our lives to Christ, we begin a process of discipleship that helps us see reality much better than before.

Pray Continually

"Pray without ceasing."
1 Thessalonians 5:17

After committing to follow Christ, we must not stop seeking His help in seeing well. Rather, we must continually seek His help, staying intimately connected to the One who can best help us see. The more we are connected to Christ, the more spiritually aware we are and the better we are able to see.

Smith Wigglesworth, a British evangelist who greatly influenced early Pentecostalism, understood the great importance of continually praying. He writes, "I hardly ever pray longer than twenty minutes, and I hardly ever go twenty minutes without praying."[2] Wigglesworth's continual reliance upon God in prayer enabled him to see what God was doing and to move with great faith.

"I hardly ever pray longer than twenty minutes, and I hardly ever go twenty minutes without praying."
—Smith Wigglesworth

Praying continually like Wigglesworth sounds impossible for most of us, and yet the Bibles exhorts us to do just that. First Thessalonians 5:17 says, "Pray without ceasing." The Greek work for "without ceasing" was also used of a continual uninterrupted cough.[3] When we face a continual cough, there are "breaks" in coughing, but the cough persists. Though not constant, there is a

137

regularity of the need to cover our mouths and to cough. So also, prayer should regularly be a part of our schedules throughout our day. As we travel, we pray. As we work on projects, we pray. Even as we engage with others in conversation, may we look to God in prayer for guidance. As we pray without ceasing, God helps us to see what steps we are to take.

The best way to start praying without ceasing is to daily set aside a regular time for God. As we spend regular times with God, inviting Him to reign in our lives, we will find Him invading our thoughts at different times during the day. Our spiritual awareness will grow, and we will see more clearly throughout our day.

Only through connecting with God through ongoing prayer can we ever hope to see the way God wants us to see. When we pray, spiritual chain reactions are catalyzed, and God gives us creativity and ideas we would not have had otherwise. When we pray, we experience "coincidences" that do not happen when we do not pray. Ongoing prayer heightens our spiritual awareness and increases our spiritual ability to see.

Jesus was our model of a life of continual prayer. At the beginning of His ministry, Jesus spent forty days in the wilderness fasting and praying, and He continued to withdraw often to lonely places to pray (Luke 4:42; 5:16). Jesus lived in constant communion with His Father, trusting Him for the ability to see everything He needed to see. Jesus declared, "I only do what I *see* my Father doing" (John 5:19). May we too be able to say, "I only do what I see my Father doing."

Seek God in Every Area of Life

Throughout our lives we are in constant need of God's help and perspective, whether engaged in perceived mundane activity or activity which is often considered more important, whether engaged in a "spiritual" activity or something more "secular."

138

Christ wants to be Lord of *every* thought, *every* decision, and *every* sphere of influence. As Abraham Kuyper writes, "No single piece of our mental world is to be hermetically sealed off from the rest, and there is not a square inch in the whole domain of our human existence over which Christ, who is Sovereign over all, does not cry: 'Mine!'"[4] God wants all of us. He wants His truth to inform every area of our lives.

We need God's help and perspective—in family life, business, education, entertainment and sports, even politics. When after four or five weeks the delegates at the Constitutional Convention in Philadelphia faced what seemed like a political impasse, the eighty-one-year-old Benjamin Franklin understood the need for God's help. He appealed for prayers for divine guidance, acknowledging the need to see political truth and reminding delegates that their prayers during the War for Independence were heard. He added that even the peace they enjoyed during the Convention was from God:

> And have we now forgotten that powerful friend? Or do we imagine that we no longer need His assistance. I have lived, Sir, a long time and the longer I live, the more convincing proofs I see of this truth—that God governs in the affairs of men. And if a sparrow cannot fall to the ground without his notice, is it probable that an empire can rise without his aid? We have been assured, Sir, in the sacred writings that "except the Lord build they labor in vain that build it." I firmly believe this; and I also believe that without his concurring aid we shall succeed in this political building no better than the Builders of Babel ... I therefore beg leave to move—that henceforth prayers imploring the assistance of Heaven, and its blessings on our deliberations, be held in this Assembly every morning before we proceed to business, and that one or more of the Clergy of this City be requested to officiate in that service.[5]

The politicians at the founding of America needed God's help to see the way forward, and we still need His help to discern what steps we should take! A. C. Dixon says,

> When we depend upon organizations, we get what organiza-tions can do; when we depend upon education, we get what

education can do; when we depend upon man, we get what man can do; but when we depend upon prayer, we get what God can do.[6]

As we seek God in every area of our lives, we give Him permission to reveal His thoughts and perspective in those areas. God wants to give clarity, but He also wants us to ask Him for the same. We have the key role of inviting Him to give insight. As we seek Him continually, He rewards (Heb 11:6) and gives wisdom (Jas 1:5).

Jesus Blesses us with Revelation

Jesus said, "I am the light of the world" (John 8:12). First John 1:5 declares, "God is light; in him there is no darkness at all." Light immensely enhances our ability to see, so it just makes sense that when we are with the Light of the world, we see much better! Not only does He show us truth, but the Light also expose lies and danger.

Time spent with Jesus allows Him to highlight things to us. As we get to know Him better, we can sense when something is emphasized or made to stand out from the ordinary. Sometimes this happens by repetition. Sometimes we just *know* that God is emphasizing something.

Jesus is a rewarder of those who seek Him (Heb 11:6), and one of the ways He rewards us is through revelation. The Greek word for revelation, *apokalupsis,* implies an unveiling or a greater ability to see. In Matthew 16, when Simon identifies Jesus as "the Christ, the Son of the living God" (v. 16), Jesus responds that Simon did not reach that conclusion with his natural abilities. Rather, Jesus says, this truth had been *revealed* to Simon by God the Father. Divine revelation was given to Simon. Jesus said, "Blessed are you, Simon Bar-Jonah! For flesh and blood has not revealed this to you, but my Father who is in heaven" (v. 17). Jesus unveils truth to us as we spend time with Him.

As we spend time with Jesus, He helps us gain His perspective and shows us steps to move forward. I cannot even begin to count the number of times God has shown something to me while I have been in prayer, seeking him. Sometimes He gives an impression to call or text someone. Other times He reminds me of a task I was supposed to do but forgot. Still other times God gives a new idea which leaves me thinking, "Why did I not think of that before now?" Over and over in my life, I have seen that as I spend time with Jesus, not only does my relationship with Him grow, but He gives me valuable revelation.

In God's Kingdom, revelation is like gold. It is extremely valuable and can be viewed as legal insider information. Revelation gives an important perspective, and pure revelation is available only from God. The Apostle Paul writes about revelation in Ephesians 1:17-18:

> [I pray] that the God of our Lord Jesus Christ, the Father of glory, may give you the Spirit of wisdom and of revelation in the knowledge of him, having the eyes of your hearts enlightened, that you may know what is the hope to which he has called you, what are the riches of his glorious inheritance in the saints.

If we want to see better, we need to spend more time with Jesus! Riches of wisdom and revelation are waiting for us. Deuteronomy 29:29 promises that "the things that are revealed belong to us and to our children forever." Proverbs 25:2 says, "It is the glory of God to conceal things, but the glory of kings is to search things out."

In God's Kingdom, revelation is like gold.

God longs to reveal His secrets to us. When we sit at the feet of Jesus and receive revelation from Him, God is providing us an eternal inheritance not only for ourselves but also our children.

How Do You See It?

1. Why is faith in Christ for salvation foundational for seeing well?

2. How can you pray without ceasing (1 Thess 5:17)? What are some first steps you can take?

3. Is there an area of life about which you really haven't been praying? God wants to be a part of every activity. Invite Him now into that area.

STRATEGY #2

FEED YOUR FAITH WITH GOD'S WORD

"Whatever keeps me from my Bible is my enemy,
however harmless it may appear to me."[1]
—*A.W. Tozer*

S everal years ago, a friend and I traveled to an area of India to pray and share the gospel. We felt prompted to stop in a small town along the road, and God connected us with Ahmed.[2] Ahmed was a person of peace—he was open to us and to the good news, and he was also very connected to his Muslim community.

On one of our trips to visit Ahmed, we spent the night in a madrasa next to Ahmed's shop and home. Madrasas in that part of Asia function both as Muslim educational institutions and homes for children who are often not fully orphans, but whose family struggles to support them.[3] Poor parents send their boys there to become "good Muslims," and more wealthy Muslims give to the madrasas as a means of *zakat* (Muslim charity).

While staying at the madrasa, about the only things we saw the boys do (besides talk with us) were to read the Koran, eat, and sleep. The only 'toy' I saw in the complex was a plastic bottle that had been made into a ball of sorts. A couple of boys did kick that back and forth a little, but not much, maybe five minutes. When I asked the boys, "How do you spend your time here?" they responded, "*Hum koran parte hai.*" (We read or study the Koran.) "And what else do you do?" I asked. "*Hum koran parte hai*" (We read or study the Koran), they replied.

There was only one light bulb in the entire compound, and it hung next to the toilet. As darkness fell and we went to sleep, my friend and I could see all the boys gathered around that single light bulb. When we woke the next morning at 5:00 a.m., the boys were once more gathered around the light bulb. Why were the boys gathered around the bulb? They needed its light to read their Korans. They read aloud from the Koran as the last thing they did at night and the first thing they did in the morning before the sun rose.

I was challenged to see the boys' dedication to the Koran, and the memory of that time in the madarsa has motivated me many times since then to be even more dedicated to the light of God's Word, the Bible. If Christ followers want to see well, we need light. Psalm 119:105 says, "Your word is a lamp to my feet and a light to my path." Along with prayer and abiding with God, perhaps the single, best thing we can do to see better spiritually is to spend time in God's Word, the primary way God communicates truth with us. His Word is inspired by God (2 Tim 3:16) and was delivered to us through people carried along by the Holy Spirit (2 Pet 1:21). It gives us tools and wisdom that we need to discern

God's desires about most things in life. Any revelation we receive from God will not contradict what He has already revealed in His Word.

The wisdom found in God's Word is essential for seeing well and interpreting the world correctly. As Tozer says, "First, the Holy Scriptures tell us what we could never learn any other way: they tell us what we are, who we are, how we got here, why we are here and what we are required to do while we remain here."[4]

God's Word also helps us see better because of the faith in Christ it ignites in our hearts. Without faith it is impossible to please God (Heb 11:6). Faith in Christ is one of the greatest filters we need as we put on our worldview glasses, and one of the best ways to grow in faith is through God's Word. Romans says, "Faith comes by hearing and hearing through the Word of God" (10:17). Hearing God raises our faith level, which is essential to please God and see well. We must ground our worldview in God's Word.

As we read God's Word, we encounter His deeds and his testimonies. We see what God has done in the past and gain faith and vision for what He wants to do today. Psalm 119:24 says, "Your testimonies are my delight; they are my counselors." The victories God gave His people in the Bible invite us to implore God to act again. They show us God's nature, His heart, and His power. They guide us and provide counsel in how to seek God.

Feed your faith, and your doubts will starve to death.

Someone has said, "Feed your faith, and your doubts will starve to death."[5] Doubts lose their strength as we focus on God and His greatness. The more we focus on how awesome God is, the less we are overwhelmed by life's circumstances. Any problem is small compared to God.

The Psalmist writes, "The unfolding of your words gives light. It imparts understanding to the simple" (Ps 119:130). We need God's light in our lives to see clearly. To grow in seeing better we must spend much time in God's Word.

Slowly Reading

Feeding your faith with God's Word can happen in a number of ways, but a key habit to develop is slowly reading through God's Word, allowing God to speak as you process the words on the page. Don't hurry through the Word. Make space for God to speak. Tune your ear to listen. As you do this, God's Spirit will highlight and emphasize things to you that He wants you to see.

When we read the Bible slowly and patiently, God's Spirit causes particular passages, phrases, or words to "jump out" at us powerfully. Sometimes we may initially feel like we are simply going through a routine, but God still uses the routine to expose us to His truth. Whenever we regularly spend time in God's Word, God increases our ability to see well spiritually.

When I was choosing an engagement ring for my wife, I remember holding up diamond rings and watching how the various stones sparkled in the light. Many rabbis view the biblical text as a gem. The more you turn it, the more the light refracts, and the more you see. God has unlimited revelation for us to discover in His Word!

> One night a group of nomads were preparing to retire for the evening when suddenly they were surrounded by a great light. They knew they were in the presence of a celestial being. With great anticipation, they awaited a heavenly message of great importance that they knew must be especially for them.
>
> Finally the voice spoke. "Gather as many pebbles as you can. Put them in your saddle bags. Travel a day's journey, and tomorrow night will find you glad, and it will find you sad."
>
> After the visitor departed, the nomads shared their disappointment and anger with each other. They had expected

146

the revelation of a great universal truth that would enable them to create wealth, health and purpose for the world. But instead, they were given a menial task that made no sense to them at all. However, the memory of the brilliance of their visitor caused each one to pick up a few pebbles and deposit them in their saddle bags while voicing their displeasure.

They traveled a day's journey, and that night while making camp, they reached into their saddle bags and discovered every pebble they had gathered had become a diamond. They were glad they had diamonds. They were sad they had not gathered more pebbles.[6]

God's Word is indeed a great treasure. It is the primary way He speaks to us. To see better, we must prioritize spending time with it. To gain God's perspective on our world and circumstances, time with His Word is paramount.

Meditation on God's Word

Meditating on God's Word is a key exercise we must practice in order to see well. The Psalmist says, "I will remember the deeds of the Lord; yes, I will remember your wonders of old. I will ponder all your work and meditate on your mighty deeds" (Ps 77:11-12). Joshua says, "This Book of the Law shall not depart from your mouth, but you shall meditate on it day and night, so that you may be careful to do according to all that is written in it. For then you will make your way prosperous, and then you will have good success" (Josh 1:8).

"Meditate" may seem like an unusual word when connected with biblical faith. We often connect meditation with Eastern religions and yoga, but the word itself simply means to focus on and reflect on something. Some people think they have never meditated. If you have ever worried, though, you have meditated—only in a negative manner. When we worry, we rehash negative thoughts and fears over and over. That is meditation! May God help us meditate in a positive manner. May He help us move His

147

truth from our heads to our hearts! May the meditation of our hearts be pleasing to God! (Ps 104:34).

Meditation for those with a biblical worldview contrasts sharply with the practice of meditation in Eastern worldviews. Buddhist and Hindu meditation often centers on trying to empty the mind. Biblical meditation focuses on filling our minds and hearts with God's truths.

Study of God's Word

A boy's grandmother was about to die and just kept reading her Bible and reading her Bible and reading her Bible. A friend asked him, "Why does your grandmother read her Bible so much?" The boy responded, "I don't know. I guess she is cramming for an exam!"

Study is an important part of gaining tools to see well. Paul exhorts Timothy, "Study to show thyself approved unto God, a workman that needeth not to be ashamed, rightly dividing the word of truth" (2 Tim 2:15, KJV). To see well, we must not only read and meditate upon God's Word, but we must also study it. We must know its contents like the back of our hands, and this requires the spiritual discipline of study. Reading is like crossing a lake on a boat, while studying is like scuba diving all over underneath the surface of the water. When we read, we want to experience the water, but we also really want to just get through it. When we study, however, we want to dive under the surface and discover treasure we can enjoy and keep. Study gives even more opportunity for understanding, which also helps us see life better.

Richard Foster defines study as follows:

[T]he mind will always take on an order conforming to the order upon which it concentrates. Perhaps we observe a tree or read a book. We see it, feel it, understand it, draw conclusions from it. And as we do, our thought processes take on an order conforming to the order in the tree or book. When this is done with concentration, perception, and repetition, ingrained habits of thought are formed.[7]

Foster further outlines four steps to study: The first is repetition, which channels the mind in a specific direction and helps ingrain habits of thought. The second step is concentration, which centers the mind and focuses attention on what is studied. The third step is comprehension, which focuses on the knowledge of the truth and provides the basis for a true perception of reality. Finally, the fourth step, reflection, helps us grasp the significance of what we are studying and see things better from God's perspective![8]

The spiritual discipline of study takes knowledge on the long journey from head to heart An African proverb says, "Knowledge is only rumor until it lives in the bones."[9] Study incorporates the Word of God into our hearts—into our bones—so it not only alters our thought patterns but transforms our minds and actions in the world. With God's Word in our hearts, we see much better!

How Do You See It?

1. How hungry are you for God's Word? What could increase your hunger?

2. Why is reading God's Word slowly at times important?

3. With regard to Scripture, how does the African proverb, "Knowledge is only rumor until it lives in the bones" resonate with you?

STRATEGY #3

LOOK BEYOND THE NATURAL, IMMEDIATE WORLD

*"[W]hat we now see did not come from
anything that can be seen."*
Hebrews 11:3b

Much of the Western world has been heavily influenced by materialism, which denies the existence of the spirit realm. Only material objects that can be physically seen are considered 'real.' Immaterial parts of our existence—like our souls and spirits—are ignored or downplayed as they cannot be scientifically observed.

Beyond the Naked or Natural Eye

In the mid-1800s, Ignaz Semmelweis was an obstetrician working at Vienna's General Hospital, an important research hospital. Semmelweis tried to get to the bottom of a horrendous mortality rate among women in the maternity ward. In the section of the maternity ward where Semmelweis practiced, the mortality rate was one in ten. Vienna General had such a frightening reputation that some women actually gave birth on the street and then went to the hospital.

The symptoms associated with these deaths in Vienna General's maternity ward—inflammation, fever, difficulty breathing—became known as "childbed fever."[1] Conventional medical science called for bleeding the patient, applying leeches, and improving air ventilation in the room. Nothing worked. More than half the women who contracted the disease died within days.

The terrible risk was well known. Semmelweis reported that patients were frequently seen "kneeling and wringing their hands,"[2] begging to be moved to a second section of the maternity ward where the mortality rate was one in fifty—still horrific, but far better than the one-in-ten rate in Semmelweis' section.

Semmelweis became obsessed with the problem. The only obvious difference between the two sections was that Semmelweis' section was attended by doctors, while the other section was attended by midwives. He could not see why that would explain the difference, so he tried to equalize every other factor among the maternity patients. He standardized everything from birthing positions to ventilation and diet to the way the laundry was done. Nothing he attempted made any measurable difference.

Then Semmelweis took a four-month leave to visit another hospital. Upon his return he discovered that in his absence the death rate had fallen significantly in his section of the ward. He did not know why, but it had definitely fallen. Gradually, his inquiry led him to think about the possible significance of doctors splitting their time between research on cadavers and the treatment of live patients. In examining his own work practices compared to those who worked for him in his absence, Semmelweis discovered that the only significant difference was that he, Semmelweis, spent far more time doing research on the cadavers.

From these observations, he developed a theory of childbed fever, a theory that became the precursor to germ theory. He concluded that "particles" from cadavers and other disease patients were being transmitted to healthy patients on the hands of the physicians. He immediately instituted a policy requiring physicians to wash their hands thoroughly in a chlorine solution before examining any patient. The death rate immediately fell to one in a hundred.[3]

The doctors were doing the best they knew how, but two hundred years ago, germs were not seen, and no one believed in them. Today people still cannot see germs without the help of microscopes or other ocular devices, yet germs are recognized as real. They are accepted by most people as the genuine causes of many types of illnesses. Their existence is only questioned by a diminishing number of people who have been isolated from modern education and life.

While few educated people in today's world deny the existence of germs, many unfortunately do deny the reality of the spirit world. Many hold a materialistic worldview, which affirms that only what is material is real. Many believe only what can be scientifically observed as reality. It is common for secularists, skeptics, and atheists to deny the existence of angels, demons, spirit beings, or even a spiritual, non-physical part of being human. Often materialists use science as an excuse for denying spiritual realities as true.

Dallas Willard warns of the danger of a materialistic worldview when he states, "The idea that knowledge—and, of course, reality—is limited to the world of the natural sciences is the single most destructive idea on the stage of life today."[4] Willard's strong statement emphasizes the damage materialistic thinking does to one's worldview. When anyone limits their worldview to what the natural sciences can demonstrate, to what can be seen with the naked eye, much of reality is lost. Vision is greatly impaired.

> ## "The idea that knowledge—and, of course, reality— is limited to the world of the natural sciences is the single most destructive idea on the stage of life today."
> *—Dallas Willard*

Faith in God enables Christ followers and other theists to see the realities of life beyond what humans can experience with their physical senses. Theists recognize there is more to life than what we can see with our physical eyes, no matter how good our vision is or how powerful our microscope may be. Theists acknowledge that what is unseen to the physical eye is as real and significant as what can be seen in the natural.

The reality of an unseen spirit world is asserted throughout the Bible. The Bible teaches us about God and His spiritual Kingdom, yet rarely gives proofs of God's existence. Why? Culturally there was little need. People in biblical times believed in God and a spiritual world. The Psalms even refer to someone who denies God's existence as a "fool" (Ps 14:1; 53:1). Instead, the Bible addresses the more pressing questions: "Who is the *true* God?" and "How can we have a relationship with the God who created us?"

Today the belief in the reality of an unseen spirit world is still common throughout the world. The existence of God and spirit beings is widely accepted in most of Latin America, Africa, and Asia. In fact, most non-Western societies believe in the spirit world. The exceptions exist in those countries where people have been discipled in materialism. Even in those countries, however, many people believe in and claim to have experienced some spiritual activity that is outside the realm of what is physically observable and quantifiable.

Not only does an unseen world exist, but it also has more importance than the physical world we see with our physical eyes. In describing the creation of the universe, Hebrews 11:3 shares that what is seen was not made from what is visible. The greater always creates the lesser, and so this verse indicates that what is unseen is even more real than what is seen, as what is unseen came first. Furthermore, Paul asserts that while our physical bodies are gradually wasting away, our spirits are not (2 Cor 4:16). He adds that material things (things seen) are transient, but things unseen are eternal (v. 18). Theists, understanding the importance of the spirit world, often consider how their actions impact this eternal realm of reality. Materialists may choose to not acknowledge anything beyond what is visible to physical eyes, but it is a choice they make. God has created every person made in His image with the capacity to know that there is more to life than just meets the eye. We can choose to acknowledge spiritual realities or pretend they do not exist.

Materialists sometime contend that they cannot believe in the spirit world or God because of a perceived lack of evidence that can be tested by science. Christ followers recognize the value of science, but they do not expect science to answer all of life's questions. Science is limited to that which is observable by the senses, while much of reality is not observable to human senses. Science cannot see the immaterial part of a human, one's soul or spirit, depending on the theist's theological view. In addition, natural sciences cannot explain consciousness, morality, love, or a human's sense of justice. Neither can science prove that a world beyond the natural world does not exist.

You Only Live Once! (But in Two Places)

"What we do in life echoes in eternity."[5]
—Maximus in the movie Gladiator

To see well, we not only need to recognize the reality of the spirit world, but we also need to acknowledge the reality of eternity and the brevity of our life on earth. As the Apostle James shares, "Our life is a vapor, a mist that appears for a little while and then vanishes" (Jas 4:14). Christ followers recognize that life on earth is fleeting, and it is the next life that really matters.

Today, YOLO ("You only live once") is a common expression. Why did you jump out of the airplane? YOLO. Why did you drive eighteen hours to attend a concert that lasts only a couple hours? YOLO. Why did you skip a work meeting to go out to eat with friends? YOLO. Too often YOLO affirms selfish behavior focused on the present. Instead, YOLO ought to inspire believers to selfless behavior focused on the future. Why? Christ followers understand that YOLO is actually true. You do only live once, but that one life lasts forever—in one of two places. We all live first on earth, and then we live either with Christ in heaven or without Christ in hell. Our one life starts here on earth, but it does not end here.

Ecclesiastes 3:11 says that God has put eternity into the human heart. Eternity is in our hearts—every person will live forever—whether we acknowledge it or not. Faith in God directs believers to live from the understanding that eternity is real, and life on earth is short. Life on earth is actually a dress rehearsal for something much greater and grander that will continue forever.

While living life here on earth, we choose whether we will spend eternity with Christ or without Him. Jesus says, "Behold, I stand at the door and knock. If anyone hears my voice and answers and lets me in, I will come into him and eat with him" (Rev 3:20). Jesus does not force anyone to choose Him. He leaves the choice to us.

Much older than YOLO is this adage: "Only one life will soon be past, only what's done for Christ will last." Believers understand that the way we live now affects the rewards we will receive later. Paul warns that the work of our lives will be tested by fire, and only that which is built upon Christ's foundation will last (1 Cor 3:13). We want to make sure we are investing for our eternal future, and one of the best ways to invest for the future is to impact other people, as they too will live for eternity. Where will our family, friends, co-workers, teachers, and neighbors live forever? When we stop and consider where Joe from work or Natalie who lives next door will spend eternity, it should affect the way we live today. What about those yet unreached with the gospel? The reality of so many unreached people groups still without access to Christ's love should impact our lifestyle. One of the greatest rewards we will experience in heaven will be meeting people who are there because of the lives we lived on earth. What a phenomenal eternal reward!

When we stop and consider where Joe from work or Natalie who lives next door will spend eternity, it should affect the way we live today.

How will we invest our time, talents, and resources during the years we live on earth? Will we use these resources to share Christ's love? Will we focus on momentary happiness and thrills, or will we set our eyes on eternal treasures? Daniel encourages us, "Those who are wise shall shine like the brightness of the day above and those who turn many to righteousness like the stars forever and ever" (Dan 12:3). May we shine like the stars forever and ever in eternity.

It is sometimes thought at funerals that the deceased person has gone from the land of the living to the land of the dead, but the opposite is actually much truer. The person who dies on earth goes from the land of the dead to the land of the living! Both my parents have entered heaven, and they are more alive now than they were when they walked on earth. They are living in perfect joy in a place more beautiful and amazing than we could ever imagine. They are reaping the rewards of living for Christ and investing in others. YOLO. You only live once. May we all live each day with eternity in our hearts!

How Do You See It?

1. According to Dallas Willard, what is the single most destructive idea on the stage of life today? Why is this belief so destructive?

2. How does believing in eternity affect your vision of life?

3. How does believing you will live forever impact your actions today?

STRATEGY #4

OVERCOME PRIDE

*"The master has failed more times
than the beginner has tried."*[1]
—Stephen McCranie

O
ne night in India we needed to travel from the city of Hardoi to Lucknow. We did not have a car, so we booked a taxi. When the taxi arrived, it did not look as if it could make it to Lucknow, but we did not have a choice. Either we had to go with the available ride or wait until the next day. We chose the available ride.

About an hour after leaving Hardoi, the sun went fully down, and darkness made headlights necessary. The driver tried to flick on the headlights, but they did not respond. No light was coming out of the front of the car. We became more and more apprehensive as the driver had to again and again jerk the steering wheel of the taxi to one side or the other in order to dodge a person or an animal. We were not sure what to do. We were in the middle of nowhere, so stopping was not much of an option, but it was dark, and our taxi had no functioning headlights!

We had no headlights, but we had two flashlights (or torches, as we call them in India). My wife and I both stuck our flashlights out the windows of the car, and we could now see about fifteen feet ahead. The light was not as strong as we would have liked, but the road and the people on it were now visible. We started missing animals and carts by greater distances. The batteries in our flashlights lasted for the next hour (another miracle!) until we reached the edge of Lucknow where there were sufficient lights to drive without headlights. We looked pretty stupid that night as we hung out the sides of the taxi holding flashlights! Who uses flashlights for headlights? We looked silly, but those flashlights kept us from rear-ending a water buffalo and a myriad of other animals, vehicles, and people. Thanks to God and two flashlights, we arrived safely home that night!

Sometimes to see more in life, we have to be willing to look foolish. In fact, if we are never willing to *look* foolish, we *are* foolish. Sometimes a very practical definition of faith is the willingness to look silly. Throughout history, God's people have made decisions that have looked foolish to people who deny God and His existence; and throughout history, God has proved himself faithful, in spite of how others perceive us.

Be Willing to Look Foolish
to See Clearly

Noah was willing to look foolish building an ark on dry land in anticipation of a "flood of waters upon the earth" (Gen 6:17). Sarah looked foolish preparing for a new baby at ninety. The Israelites looked foolish marching around Jericho blowing trumpets. David looked foolish attacking Goliath with a slingshot. The Magi looked foolish following a star. Peter looked foolish stepping out of a boat in the middle of a lake. Jesus looked foolish hanging naked on the Cross.

God seldom shows us a complete plan of what He wants us to do. To see more, we have to be willing to step out in what He does show us.

Those who see with faith have the humility needed to look foolish in the process of obedience. People of faith understand that those around them probably will not see what they are seeing and that they may be ridiculed in the process of obedience. Yet, there is a willingness to move forward anyway, and the results speak for themselves, don't they? Noah and his family were saved from the flood. Sarah gave birth to Isaac. The walls of Jericho came tumbling down. David defeated Goliath. The Magi found the Messiah. Peter walked on water. And Jesus rose from the dead. Do you know why some people have never killed a giant or walked on water? It's at least partially because they are not willing to look foolish. They are not willing to attack with a slingshot or get out of the boat in the middle of the lake.

God seldom shows us a complete plan of what He wants us to do. To see more, we have to be willing to step out into what He does show us. That can feel very awkward at times. Others can accuse us of not being polished—and they might be right—but God is more concerned about our openness to roll with what He shows us than our looking put together and polished.

Be Ready to Deal with Stigma

We also need humility to deal with the stigma that inevitably comes with attempting to see more. As we walk in faith with God, He often prompts us to do unusual things. Sometimes those actions may not be perceived as "cool" or "respectable" in the eyes of friends and mainstream culture. We may suffer the loss of status in some circles. Are we willing to pay the price of stigma?

I love the saying, "Pursue God—not the odd!" Yet, sometimes those seeking to see what God is doing are perceived as odd. People laughed at Jesus as He went to raise the dead (Mark 5:40). They mocked Him over and over from Pilate's court to the whipping stand to the Cross.

The word "stigma" is linguistically related to the Latin word *stigmata*, which refers to the stripes or whipping that Jesus endured. Jesus, for the joy set before Him, endured the whipping, the shame, and the Cross (Heb 12:2). As R. T. Kendall notes, "Every generation has its stigma by which the believer's faith is tested. Yesterday's stigma is easily accepted today. We may think we are being sufficiently open to God merely because we accept yesterday's stigma."[2] Today's Church, though, must be willing to face the unique stigma of our time.

When God gives revelation, He expects obedience. Often obedience to God leads us to actions that may set us apart as being different or feeling stigmatized. Our willingness to endure this stigmatization allows us to receive even more revelation from God. It is a price believers often must pay for the revelation God provides.

Be Willing to Ask for Help to See

Benno Muller-Hill, a professor in the University of Cologne's genetics department, tells how one morning in high school he stood last in a line of forty students in the schoolyard. His physics teacher had set up a telescope so his students could view a planet and its moons. The first student stepped up to the telescope. He looked through it, but when the teacher asked if he could see anything, the boy replied, "No." His nearsightedness hampered his view. The teacher showed him how to adjust the focus, and the boy finally said he could see the planet and moons. One by one, the students stepped up to the telescope and saw what they were supposed to see. Finally, the second to last student looked into the telescope and announced that he could not see anything.

"You idiot," shouted the teacher, "you have to adjust the lenses."

The student tried, but he finally said, "I still can't see anything. It is all black."

The teacher, disgusted, looked through the telescope himself and then looked up with a strange expression. He quickly glanced at the end of the telescope—the lens cap still covered the telescope. *None* of the students had been able to see anything![3]

We need humility to ask for help from others when we cannot see well. We need to admit when we are confused and lost. We need to be humble enough to ask a second, third, and fourth time if necessary. We will discuss getting help from others in Key #5, but it is first important to emphasize the importance of humbling ourselves enough to ask for help. Help may come in the form of wisdom or information that gives a different perspective. Help may be feedback about our ideas and plans. Help may be the suggestion of a resource for seeing an issue better. May we not let pride keep us from going to others who can give us better perspective.

May we not let pride keep us from going to others who can give us better perspective.

Some issues are harder than others to get help in seeing. As I write this chapter, America is going through another difficult season of race relations. Members of different ethnic groups often see the same circumstances and events differently. As members of the body of Christ, we need each other's perspectives. We need to be willing to ask others to help us see from their point of view. Having genuine, tough conversations takes humility.

Often the enemy uses pride to keep us from interacting with the very people who are best equipped to help us see. Several years ago, I was church planting in Asia and needed insight regarding multiplying house churches. A particular leader knew much more than me, but I did not want to approach him because of my pride and some organizational differences. Eventually I did meet with the leader, and I gained valuable perspective. If I had let pride rule, I would have missed seeing several things that later led to more fruitful church planting. May God help us to remain humble, so we can see more clearly in His Kingdom!

How Do You See It?

1. How does humility enable you to see better?

2. What types of stigmas have you experienced as you follow Christ and attempt to see clearly?

3. Has pride ever kept you from asking for help in seeing? When or how?

STRATEGY #5

PURSUE GRATITUDE

"Today is a gift. That's why it's called the present."
— *Alice Morse Earle*[1]

People with a wide range of worldviews recognize the impact that thanksgiving has on our attitude. Thanksgiving does much more than give us a better attitude, though; it helps us see better spiritually. As we pay attention to God's blessings and give thanks, we grow in our ability to notice things around us. Things we may have taken for granted get more attention when we prioritize thankfulness. Choosing gratitude means choosing greater alertness to our surroundings.

G. K. Chesterton said that his "ultimate goal in life was to take nothing for granted—not a sunrise, not a flower, not a laugh."[2] What a great goal—to be grateful for absolutely everything! Unfortunately, we often do not live up to this standard. We often take for granted that which we already have. When we are healthy, we take our health for granted. When we are wealthy, we take our wealth for granted. When things are going well, we tend to take our circumstances for granted. That is how human nature usually works, and it is a trap of the enemy. As Max Lucado notes, "The devil doesn't have to steal anything from you; all he has to do is make you take it for granted."[3]

"The devil doesn't have to steal anything from you; all he has to do is make you take it for granted."
—*Max Lucado*

The Danger of Complaining

Another trick of the devil is to tempt us to focus on the negatives in our situation. In anyone's story, there is always a positive. Alphonse Karr writes, "Some people are always grumbling because roses have thorns. I am thankful that thorns have roses."[4]

Although grumbling and complaining displease God, thankfulness actually attracts His presence. As the Psalmist writes, "I will enter His gates [His presence] with thanksgiving in my heart" (Ps 100:4). As we thank God, we attract greater measures of His presence. Eugene Peterson paraphrases Psalm 100:4 in this way: "Enter with the password: 'Thank you!'" When we are thankful, it is as if the door swings open and God says, "Come into my presence. Make yourself at home." Then, as we sit in His presence, we are transformed, and we gain His perspective.

Born as a slave, George Washington Carver could have complained about many things in life, yet he exhibited consistent gratitude to God, which helped Carver see more clearly in life. Carver once asked God to explain to him why He made the universe; he shared that the Lord declined answering his question. Then Carver asked God, "Tell me what man was made for."

The Lord answered, "Little man, you are still asking for more than you can handle. Cut down the extent of your request and improve the intent."

After some time, Carver asked, "Mr. Creator, why did You make the peanut?"

"That's better!" the Lord said, and He gave me a handful of peanuts and went with me back to the laboratory and, together, we got down to work."[5]

Carver was grateful for the challenge he received from God, and he often prayed before entering his lab: "Open thou mine eyes that I may behold wondrous things out of thy law."[6] Despite the struggles he faced in life, Carver chose to be thankful to God. This attitude enabled Carver to discover many things about God's creation. When he was done studying the peanut, Carver had discovered more than 265 products that could be made with that tiny bit of God's world.[7]

Seeing the Miracles around Us

Gratitude further helps us see God's hand working everyday miracles around us. As we maintain a heart of thankfulness, we tend to notice things we might otherwise overlook. We take less for granted.

A man and his dog are walking along a beach when they come upon another visitor at the beach. The owner of the dog is proud of his dog's newly mastered feat, so he says to the visitor, "Watch this!" He tosses a piece of driftwood far out into the sea, and the dog immediately runs on top of the ocean, fetches the wood and runs back. The visitor just shakes his head in disbelief, whereupon the owner repeats the trick two more times. Finally, the man asks the visitor, "Did you notice anything unusual?" The visitor responds, "Your dog can't swim, can he?" Instead of being amazed at a dog walking on water, the visitor chose to complain about the dog not swimming. Some people refuse to see miracles no matter how obvious they are.

Thanksgiving is a spiritual weapon that helps us count our blessings and intentionally notice things we may otherwise take for granted.

Einstein said, "There are only two ways to live your life. One is as though nothing is a miracle. The other is as though everything is a miracle."[8] The first way leads to complacency and boredom; the second way leads us to joyful observation and expectation. Taking things for granted is a human tendency that dulls our spiritual perception. It has been said that if we do not count our blessings, we discount them. Thanksgiving is a spiritual weapon that helps us count our blessings and intentionally notice things we may otherwise take for granted. Thanksgiving helps us see what God has done and is doing and to remain better in tune with the Spirit of God.

Removing Distortion Due to Envy

Gratitude further helps us to overcome another vision distortion tool of the enemy: envy. Envy is counting another's blessings instead of one's own. It poisons our thoughts and pushes us to focus on what others have rather than on the blessings God has given us. Envious people fixate on the advantages and possessions others enjoy. Envy encourages anger at perceived injustices. It is fed by the comparison game, and in the comparison game, no one wins. The Apostle Paul makes it clear comparing ourselves to others is not wise a wise practice (2 Cor 10:12). Comparison blinds us to the blessings God has given us. It coaxes us to forget the testimonies of God's kindness and faithfulness in our lives. It robs us of an honest perspective regarding God's hand on our lives and families.

Gratitude does the opposite. Gratitude helps us recognize the unique blessings God has given to us. Thankful people focus on their blessings versus the perceived better benefits someone else has received. Instead of longing for what seem to be the greener pastures of others, thankful people root their souls in what helps to keep them present in their circumstances. Gratitude helps people remember that even if the grass does seem to look greener on the other side, that grass also has to be mowed, fertilized, watered, and probably weeded.

Envy is counting another's blessings instead of one's own.

Thankful for and Working with What We Have

Burdened for the children of tenant farmers and poor landowners who did not have access to quality education, Martha Berry decided to open a school. After founding the Berry School near Rome, Georgia, Martha spent a lot of time fundraising. She was quite good at it and connected with many wealthy donors.

Martha once asked Henry Ford for one million dollars to assist her school. He coolly gave her a dime instead. Martha graciously accepted the dime and then used it to buy some peanuts for her schoolboys to plant. The next season they used the entire crop of peanuts to plant a larger field. Eventually they sold enough peanuts to buy a school piano. Martha then wrote a letter to Mr. Ford thanking him for the donation and telling him what his dime had done. Ford was deeply impressed and invited her to Detroit where he gave her the afore requested one million dollars.[9] Instead of taking offense at Ford's initial gift of the dime, Martha chose to be thankful. Her gratefulness enabled her to have unclouded vision to know how to multiply the dime.

Gratitude helps us focus on what is right instead of what is wrong, on what we have instead of what we do not have.

Gratitude helps us focus on what is right instead of what is wrong, on what we have instead of what we do not have. King David counseled himself, "Praise the Lord, O my soul, and *do not forget his benefits*" (Ps 103:2, italics added). When we focus on God's benefits and blessings, we are clearing our gaze. We are cleaning the lenses, so to speak, through which we see our world. Starting from a place of gratitude allows us to see God and His purposes more clearly.

How Do You See It?

1. How does thanksgiving help us see more clearly?

2. How does gratitude help us overcome the distortion of envy?

3. Consider a time you have recently complained. What are three things you can be thankful for in that situation?

STRATEGY #6

GAIN PERSPECTIVE FROM CHRIST'S BODY

"The eye cannot say to the hand, 'I have no need of
you,' nor again the head to the feet,
'I have no need of you.'"
1 Corinthians 12:21

harles "Tremendous" Jones, a successful businessman and
best-selling author, used to say that the only difference
between who you are today and the person you will be in
five years will come from the books you read and the people with
whom you associate."[1] To see better, we need to read books that
teach us how to see God and what He is doing. The Bible is the
best place to start! We also need to spend time with people who
see well! Hanging out with people who have good track records
for spiritual perception will impact us. A professional speaker

once quipped, "My friends didn't believe that I could become a successful speaker. So, I did something about it. I went out and found me some new friends!" People we spend time with influence us, either positively or negatively. Evaluate your friends and mentors. We need to seek out people who share a passion for seeing well and wanting others to see well. We all need positive encouragement in the right direction.

Mentors with Good Vision

A young man sitting by the riverbank was discouraged since he could not swim across the river. An elderly man walked up, rolled up his pants, and then walked across the surface of the water. The young man was in disbelief until another elderly man arrived, rolled up his pants, and also walked across the surface of the water. Eventually, a third elderly man arrived and did the same thing! Finally, the young man decided to try for himself. He rolled up his pants and tried to walk across the surface of the water—only to sink and be carried away by the swift current. The three elderly men looked back and replied, "If only he had asked us—we could have told him where the stones were placed to cross over the river safely!"[2]

Seek out people who can mentor you in discerning God's ways and seeing with God's perspective. Ask people who are gifted in seeing well to help you learn how to see better. We do not need to learn how to see well by ourselves. Many other followers of Christ have gone before us and can give us insight, if we will make the effort to reach out and ask them for help. If we are a young "Timothy," we need an experienced "Paul" to help us learn. If we are a more experienced "Paul," we should be helping a young Timothy. The Kingdom wins when mentors help others to improve their sight.

In our quest to see better, mentors offer valuable feedback and input. Often, we are actually seeing more than we realize, but we need someone to affirm that what we are sensing is on track. We need people with whom we can test our perceptions safely. Sometimes we are wrong or "off," and in those times, we need trustworthy people who can encourage us in the right direction. "Experience is the best teacher" is a common expression. More accurate, though, is "Guided or evaluated experience is the best teacher." We learn best not just by experience, but by wise feedback in the process.

> "Experience is the best teacher" is a common expression. More accurate, though, is "Guided or evaluated experience is the best teacher."

Often what is needed most from mentors is not advice, but support, encouragement, and companionship. Most people already know what they need to work on. Most people need support. They want to know they do not have to navigate the difficulties of life on their own. We always need friends who will encourage us to keep seeking the Lord for spiritual insight.

Honor Leaders

"Pay to all what is owed to them ... respect to whom respect is owed, honor to whom honor is owed."
Romans 13:7

As we connect with Christ's Body, we need to honor leaders whom God has put in our lives. People in positions of authority often have information and perspectives that we do not have. They can help us see better if we give them the honor called for by their positions and if we ask for their help.

People in institutional leadership have viewpoints others do not have. Their perceptions can be a great blessing to us if we are humble and submissive. A leader's insight can become ours if we honor that leader and his or her role. Many times in my life I have sought the guidance of my leaders and received direction in what to do. Is it possible that occasionally those leaders were wrong in some way? Is it possible that they were at times affected by wrong motives or that sometimes a better option existed? Yes, to all of these questions, but leaders are accountable before God for their leadership, and God is big enough to use even broken people to direct us in the way we should go. I can say with great confidence that God is always faithful, and He has often used appointed leaders to give me and my family godly insight and direction.

A leader's insight can become ours if we honor that leader and his or her role.

Honor All Members of the Body

"The cow does not know the value of its tail
until it cuts it off."
—*African proverb (Igbo)*

Paul writes in 1 Corinthians, "We have the mind of Christ" (2:16c). He does not write, "*I* have the mind of Christ," or "*You* have the mind of Christ." Rather, Paul writes that together "*We* have the mind of Christ" (emphasis added).

We see much better when we are connected with Christ's Body. God gives some revelation to all of His children, but not all of His revelation to just some of His children. He gives pieces of revelation to each one of us, but He does not reveal all to just one person. Part of the reason for this is to keep us humble. No believer is a "know-it-all"—even though some may act like it! We are all designed to be interdependent upon each other and the

174

Holy Spirit. No part of the Body can say it does not need the other parts (1 Cor 12:21).

There is an apocryphal story of a man asking God about heaven and hell. God said to the man, "Come, I will show you hell."

They entered a room where a group of people sat around a huge pot of stew. Everyone was famished, desperate, and starving. Each held a spoon that reached the pot, but each spoon's handle was so much longer than the person's own arm that it could not be used to get the stew into their mouths. The suffering in hell was horrific.

"Come, now I will show you heaven," God said after a while. They entered another room, identical to the first—the pot of stew, a group of people, the same long-handled spoons. But in this room, everyone was happy and well-nourished.

"I do not understand," said the man. "Why are they happy here when they were miserable in the other room? Everything is the same."

God smiled. "Ah, that is easy," He said. "Here in heaven everyone sees the value of each other, and they have learned to feed each other." The man then realized that each person was using his or her spoon to feed stew to someone else.[3]

To see well, we need to see our need for each other and engage with others in Christ's Body. Everyone benefits when we act as a body instead of as individual members concerned only about our own needs. God has given us gifts and revelation that others need, and other people have gifts and insight that we need.

When we honor and value people, we posture ourselves to learn from them and gain insight. Conversely, it is difficult to learn from anyone if we look down on them. We must be open to God using anyone to teach us about seeing better in life. We can even learn from people with whom we do not agree. When sitting in meetings where people are sharing things you disagree with, ask the Lord about it. "God, if I were speaking about this topic, what would you have me share? And what is something I can learn by listening to this person?" It is amazing what God can reveal as we remain teachable!

Position Yourself in Growth Environments

Along with the ongoing process of learning and growing in our normal context, God also uses special events and encounters to help us see better. Sometimes we can gain new insight for seeing well by making a trip to an event, a conference, or a church besides our home church. Sometimes God wants to use another part of the Body of Christ to aid us in our ability to see.

In the late 1990s, thousands of believers travelled to Pensacola, FL, to be a part of the Pensacola Revival. My family waited in line all day long to get inside Brownsville Assembly of God to hear Steve Hill preach and Michael Brown give a prophetic word. The presence of the Lord was strong, and many people responded for salvation that evening.

Even back then there were many voices asking, "Why should I go to Brownsville Assembly of God?" "Isn't God *here* just He is in Pensacola?" Yes, God is everywhere, and whatever He can do in Pensacola or wherever else you might go, He *can* do right where you are in your hometown. Yet sometimes God chooses to move supernaturally in particular times and places. Sometimes He does this in places different from our "normal" environment. Purposefully placing ourselves in a new environment or setting may help our capacity to see. Being intentional and willing to go somewhere new reveals our hunger to God, and God is a rewarder of those who seek Him.

During revivals God can give us a new level of spiritual sight. Revivals can and should happen anywhere. For some reason, though, they do not. Is it wrong to make a journey to a location that is experiencing revival? If I live, for example, in St. Louis, is it wrong to go to Des Moines to attend a revival meeting? The answer to both of these questions is no, not if we sense God's peace about traveling to another location.

Why do we sometimes receive more at a special event or conference than we do in our normal routine and place of worship? Sometimes we are more open to receiving something new in a special meeting. Sometimes being anonymous enables us to respond with more openness. Sometimes God does empower people in a unique way, and that empowerment is for a particular location and time. Sometimes God first gives a special anointing, revelation, or spiritual gift to someone in one city, with the plan for it to spread elsewhere. The intensity of revival may indeed be stronger in the original location for a period of time, but genuine moves of God are meant to spread.

The Magi were willing to travel a long distance at great expense to experience Christ the New King. Today wise men and women still travel to see the King better. Maybe you should consider a trip to grow in clarity of vision!

Today wise men and women still travel to see the King better.

As we seek to see more, we need the perspectives of others. God never designed us to see everything by ourselves. Together we are the body of Christ, and together we have the mind of Christ.

How Do You See It?

1. Who are people in your life with whom you can spend more time to get fresh perspective?

2. Why is honoring all members of the Body of Christ important for gaining perspective?

3. Have you ever traveled to a conference or new location to encounter God? How did that impact your spiritual life and ability to see?

STRATEGY #7

SEEK THE BAPTISM OF THE HOLY SPIRIT

*"God is looking for [people] through whom
He can do the impossible—what a pity that we plan
only the things we can do by ourselves."[1]*
—A.W. Tozer

R ight before Jesus gave the Great Commission and ascended
to heaven, He told His disciples to wait in Jerusalem until
they were clothed with power from on high (Luke 24:49,
Acts 1:4). Jesus knew that the disciples would need His power to
do the work He had commissioned them to do. He never meant for
them to try to do the impossible (i.e., disciple nations, proclaim
the gospel to all nations, cast out demons, heal the sick) without

the power of the Holy Spirit. To see the impossible happen, He knew they needed the Holy Spirit's power!

God's indwelling, revelatory Spirit lives in all believers upon salvation (Rom 8:9b, 14) and gives them new spiritual eyes, enabling them to see better spiritually. In Acts 1:8, though, Jesus promises even more: "But you will receive power when the Holy Spirit has come upon you, and you will be my witnesses in Jerusalem and in all Judea and Samaria, and to the ends of the earth." The Holy Spirit was already living within the disciples when Jesus spoke these words. Jesus had already died and risen from the grave, and He had already told the disciples to "Receive the Holy Spirit" (John 20:22c). Yet Jesus wanted His disciples to experience more of the Holy Spirit. He knew they needed the Holy Spirit to come *upon* them.

In Acts 2:3-4 we see the fulfillment of Jesus' promise given in Acts 1:8: "And divided tongues as of fire appeared to them and rested on each one of them. And they were all filled with the Holy Spirit and began to speak in other tongues as the Spirit gave them utterance." According to verse 14, Peter stands in front of Jews from every nation, prophetically proclaiming the good news of Jesus. That day about three thousand people responded to the Spirit-empowered ministry of Peter (Acts 2:41). On the Day of Pentecost, God poured out His Spirit in a powerful way upon the believers, and God has been pouring out His Spirit ever since.

The Holy Spirit knows all things and wants to empower all believers with accurate spiritual sight. While the Holy Spirit dwells in every follower of Christ, the experience of the baptism of the Holy Spirit gives us even more connection with God, more revelation, and more empowerment. All of this leads to even better spiritual vision.

Acts 1:8 indicates that the baptism of the Holy Spirit is primarily for having power for witnessing in both nearby and far locations. Missionaries have long emphasized the need for Spirit empowerment to see breakthroughs in people groups around the world. God demonstrates the Spirit's power in many ways, including healings, deliverances, *and* a greater measure of spiritual perception and connection to the Holy Spirit.

In a natural war, good intelligence or information is needed to increase the effectiveness of other types of weapons. Soldiers in a physical war need to perceive where to go, see where to aim, etc. Good intelligence and direction are required in spiritual warfare too. The Holy Spirit provides believers with good intelligence by revealing things not previously understood or known. God's revelation helps believers see better spiritually.

Luke's Biblical Pattern

Denzil Miller notes Luke's pattern in Acts 2:4-41; 10:45-46; and 19:6 as (1) the Holy Spirit falling upon people, (2) Spirit-inspired speech in tongues, and then (3) Spirit-inspired speech in the vernacular of the people.[2] In step three of each of these passages, Spirit-inspired speech is also accompanied by Spirit-inspired revelation from God needed to give Spirit-inspired speech in the vernacular of the people.

In Acts 2:4 the Holy Spirit came upon the disciples, and they began to speak in other tongues as the Spirit gave them utterance. Words were given to the disciples by the Spirit, and the disciples spoke those words aloud. The next verse recounts that devout Jews from many nations of the diaspora were present and wondered at the words spoken. They saw unschooled people speaking and heard them speak in languages that had not been learned through study. Then they heard Peter prophetically proclaiming truths from Scripture that the Holy Spirit had revealed to him.

In Acts 10 Peter proclaims the gospel to Gentiles and sees the Spirit fall on all who heard the word. The Jews with Peter confirm the outpouring of the Holy Spirit when they hear the

Gentiles speaking in tongues and praising God in an unknown language! The Gentiles had received the Holy Spirit just as the Jewish people had.

In Acts 19 Paul was in Ephesus ministering to the believers, and God baptized them with the Holy Spirit. They too began speaking in tongues and also prophesied. The baptism of the Holy Spirit helped the disciples not only speak in languages they did not understand (tongues), but they also grew in spiritual perception. They received revelation to prophesy. We will discuss the gift of prophecy more in Strategy #8, but for now the point is that revelation (spiritual perception/seeing) is part of the process of prophesying. The baptism of the Holy Spirit often helps us see better spiritually so we can better speak for God.

Tim Enloe shares an illustration about a donut to teach about the baptism of the Holy Spirit. A doughnut can be injected with chocolate, so there is plenty of filling inside. While the donut has a good bit of chocolate inside, still more can happen to the donut! The doughnut can be dipped or baptized with chocolate. After being baptized with chocolate, the doughnut is not only filled, but overflowing with chocolate, and chocolate gets all over anything it touches.

We need more of the Holy Spirit in our lives. Every believer needs the baptism of the Holy Spirit. The more we have of the Holy Spirit, the more potential we have to spiritually see. A sinner far from God sees their sinful spiritual state when God's Spirit touches them. Believers see or sense God's love in a stronger manner when the Holy Spirit is working in their lives. Believers can also see next steps of obedience when the Holy Spirit descends upon them, and they know better what to speak when they receive revelation from God.

Tongues as a Revelatory Tool

Speaking in tongues is the initial sign of being baptized in the Holy Spirit, but it is also a tool God gives us for growing in spiritual sensitivity. As the Apostle Paul notes in 1 Corinthians 14:4, "The one who speaks in a tongue builds up himself." Paul is not talking about growing physically taller or gaining more muscle mass. He is recognizing the role that speaking in tongues has on our spirits. Speaking in tongues is like spiritual weightlifting. When we speak in tongues, our spirits grow in their capacity to perceive God and His promptings. Paul clearly saw the great value of speaking in tongues because he proclaimed that he spoke in tongues more than all the Corinthian believers (1 Cor 14:18).

Speaking in tongues further helps us be more aware of the Holy Spirit in our lives and helps us trust God more. Often when we speak in tongues, we can sense God's Spirit more upon us. We also grow in our trust in God—we cannot physically see the Holy Spirit, but we sense His work in our lives. We trust Him to help us see what we could not see without His help.[3]

When tongues are interpreted, they give greater spiritual insight. Paul urges believers to seek the interpretation of what God speaks through the gift of tongues (1 Cor 14:13). This is especially critical in group settings. Receiving an interpretation of what was spoken in tongues can also be a great encouragement in smaller settings or when alone with God.

In addition to the baptism of the Holy Spirit, all believers need constant new fillings of the Holy Spirit. Paul encourages the Ephesians to not get drunk with wine but to "be filled with the Spirit" (Eph 5:18). As ever-growing spiritual vessels, we need ongoing infillings of the Holy Spirit so we can continually see more clearly.

Gateway Experience

The baptism of the Holy Spirit is a gateway to other gifts of the Spirit. Once believers have been baptized in the Spirit, they can expect a greater release of spiritual gifts in their lives. Something about the process of humbling ourselves before God and surrendering our tongues to speak in languages we do not understand positions us to grow and operate in spiritual gifts.

According to Gordon Anderson,

the baptism in the Holy Spirit is significant additional power for life and ministry given by God subsequent to salvation. ... This experience results in added faith in God, increased power and gifts for ministry, increased emotion and passion, and an enhanced awareness of the experiential dimension of God's presence in the life of the Pentecostal believer.[4]

Miller notes that every Christian must face the question, "In what measure do I want to see the gifts of the Spirit operative in my own life and ministry?"[5] This question will inevitably lead to the issue of Spirit baptism. Jesus commanded His disciples to wait until they had received power from on high (Luke 24:49). Any believer wanting to grow in spiritual revelation must take seriously the final command of Jesus to be baptized in the Holy Spirit (Acts 1:4-5).

How Do You See It?

1. Have you been baptized in the Holy Spirit with the evidence of speaking in tongues? If so, how often do you pray in tongues?

2. If you have not been baptized in the Holy Spirit with the evidence of speaking in tongues, God wants to baptize you! The baptism of the Holy Spirit is not something we earn or are ever worthy of receiving. It is a gift from God for every believer! You may seek this gift on your own, but asking a spiritual leader to help you (see Strategy #6) honors them and gives you more perspective and encouragement in the journey. Reading Acts is also helpful.

3. Paul shares in 1 Corinthians 14:4 that as we speak in tongues, we build ourselves up spiritually. While we are all built up, everyone's experience is different. How do you feel when you speak in tongues?

STRATEGY #8

DESIRE SPIRITUAL GIFTS

"Pursue love and earnestly desire the spiritual gifts, especially that you may prophesy."
1 Corinthians 14:1

S uraj and Sam went to the mall and met Abdi[1] sitting at a table. Suraj had a word of knowledge for Abdi that he had been injured in an accident, and Suraj knew that God wanted to heal and deliver Abdi. So Suraj asked Abdi about his condition. Abdi then confirmed that he did have a physical problem that was hindering him from working and that he did want to be healed. Suraj and Sam prayed on the spot for Abdi's healing, and God removed all the pain and movement restrictions from Abdi's injury. They were then able to pray with Abdi for salvation.

Spiritual gifts bless the body of Christ and help believers see better in the process. Words of knowledge, the gift of faith, the gift of wisdom, prophecy, and other spiritual gifts all help Christ followers to spiritually perceive more. They also help us as we assist others in seeing what God is doing and wants to do in their lives.

Words of Knowledge

Words of knowledge help believers perceive things they cannot see with their own natural abilities. These words of knowledge then open the door for God to encourage, heal, or do other heart work. Sometimes words of knowledge come by God speaking a word in one's heart. Other times, God gives a mental picture. Still other times, God may cause our bodies to feel pain or other sensations as a means of giving a word of knowledge. Words of knowledge may also come through dreams or just inexplicably "knowing" something, often quite randomly. God shares words of knowledge in many ways, and it is part of discipleship to learn to understand God's unique language with us as believers.

One of the first times I discerned a word of knowledge from God happened as I walked on a street in Kolkata, India. I sensed God's presence in a unique way, and then my leg started hurting. A Muslim man was walking next to me, and I asked if he had any pain in his leg. He looked shocked, but replied, "Yes." Then this man agreed to let me pray for him, and God took away all the pain. Again shocked, the man asked what had just happened, giving me an open door to share the Gospel right there on the street. Words of knowledge open all kinds of doors for Kingdom impact!

The Gift of Faith

The gift of faith mentioned in 1 Corinthians 12:9 goes beyond normal salvific faith, which every believer has. The gift of faith is given by God at key moments when believers need to see God's heart in a special way. Often the gift of faith gives revelation of God's power and desire to work in a particular circumstance. It helps us know what God wants to do and that He *can* do it.

In the Spring of 2020, the COVID-19 pandemic shut down just about every group activity around the world. The Antioch Initiative[2] had previously planned Run for the Unreached, our annual advocacy run for people groups still without access to the gospel, to happen in April. In the natural it looked like the event needed to be cancelled (everything else around our university and city was being cancelled). Through a series of events, God spoke and released a gift of faith to believe for things to still go forward virtually. Prior to the pandemic, the goal was for 200 people to participate in the physical event. With the gift of faith and God's favor, over 500 people participated virtually! Through faith we can see more done in our lives and communities than could ever be done through our own strength or ability.

The Gift of Wisdom

The gift of wisdom (1 Cor 12:8) is another gift Jesus gives that helps with spiritual perception. This spiritual gift may not seem "spiritual" at times. It may not be flashy, but it is definitely a gift to be desired. Going beyond "normal" wisdom, the gift of wisdom exceeds natural learning and experience and is an important way God helps believers see solutions to difficult problems.

Generally speaking, while a word of knowledge shows us information, a word of wisdom helps us see how to *use* that information. Wisdom applies knowledge in a godly way. Some examples in Acts include the decision of the apostles to select deacons to serve the physical needs of the widows (Acts 6:1-7), the decision of the Jerusalem Council to not require Gentile believers to be circumcised (15:13-21), and Paul's use of his Roman citizenship for a Kingdom cause (16:35-40).[3] The gift of wisdom allows believers to see how to apply Scripture and to see godly ways to address situations so the Kingdom of God advances.

189

The Gift of Prophecy

The gift of prophecy is a divine empowerment to speak for God, yet it also can help believers see better spiritually. How does a speaking gift help one to see better? Part of the process of speaking for God is first receiving revelation from God. The revelation He gives may come in many ways, including hearing, feeling, smelling, touching, and *seeing*. There are many ways God can speak to us prophetically through seeing, but one example includes seeing something in the natural world and spiritually knowing there is a spiritual significance to what we are seeing. One of the Hebrew words for prophet, *chozeh* (or *ho-zeh*), is also translated as "seer," a person who sees what God wants to communicate.

In Jeremiah 1:11, God asks Jeremiah, "Jeremiah, what do you see?" Jeremiah responds that he sees an almond branch. The word for "almond" in Hebrew sounds like the word for "watching." So, God responds, "You have seen well, for I am watching over my word to perform it" (v. 12). God spoke to Jeremiah through Jeremiah's seeing a natural almond tree. Another example of how prophecy helps us to see better is in the following verse (v. 13). God asks Jeremiah again, "What do you see?" Jeremiah responds, "I see a boiling pot, facing away from the north." Jeremiah probably did not see an actual physical pot. He was probably seeing a spiritual picture or vision of a pot. Yet, God used this spiritual picture or vision that Jeremiah saw to prophetically speak again. "Out of the north disaster shall be let loose upon all the inhabitants of the land" (v. 14). This prophecy was in reference to Jerusalem's being invaded from the North.

Prophecy is a spiritual gift that can be used to see better and minister more effectively in almost any setting. Many Christ followers have prophesied in church services to encourage believers, but God has been using believers more and more to prophesy outside the walls of church buildings. Many times, God has given me a word to share with a waiter, taxi driver, or store attendant. God wants to speak to people in most any context. Recently I have seen God use believers prophesying over people on the streets of our city. God can use prophecy anywhere! This gift is available to all believers, which encourages the Body of Christ and helps it grow in spiritual perception. Believers are exhorted to desire spiritual gifts, especially prophecy (1 Cor 14:1). Paul shares that all believers can prophesy one by one so all may learn and be encouraged (v. 31). As we grow in prophecy, we often grow in our ability to spiritually see as well. May God help us earnestly desire to prophesy!

Paul York notes that there are two ways a disciple may bear witness for Christ.[4] First, he or she can speak to people about God, and this is good, but a better way is for God to speak through him or her to people![5] God speaking through us to another person is another definition of prophecy, and as we prophesy, God sharpens our spiritual vision by giving revelation and speaks through us to people needing His words.

> ## "There are two ways a disciple may bear witness for Christ. First, he or she can speak to people about God, and this is good, but a better way is for God to speak through him or her to people."
> *–Paul York*

Christians are commanded to earnestly desire spiritual gifts. These gifts are a great benefit to the body of Christ, helping us navigate life with greater clarity. May we seek Jesus and the gifts He has for us!

Discernment Based on God's Word

As Christians grow in using spiritual gifts and develop their ability to see in the spiritual realm, they will need more and more discernment. The Apostle John admonishes:

> Beloved, do not believe every spirit, but test the spirits to see whether they are from God, for many false prophets have gone out into the world. By this you know the Spirit of God: every spirit that confesses that Jesus Christ has come in the flesh is from God, and every spirit that does not confess Jesus is not from God. This is the spirit of the antichrist, which you heard was coming and now is in the world already (1 John 4:1-3).

First Corinthians 12:10 lists discerning of spirits as a spiritual gift. The word in Greek is in the plural form, suggesting that there are many ways discernment is needed. The gift of discernment is especially valuable with the gift of prophecy. As we receive prophecy or other revelation, we need to discern the source. Is its source heavenly, human, or hell? We need the gift of discernment to recognize the difference. Hebrews 5:14 lets us know that discernment is developed by continual training: "Solid food is for the mature, for those who have their powers of discernment trained by constant practice to distinguish good from evil." By practicing discernment, we become more mature and able to distinguish between God and the enemy's voices.

A banker who had reached the age of retirement was about to be replaced by a young man. Upon his arrival to take the helm from his predecessor, the younger man asked the older man how he had become successful.

The man replied, "Good decisions."
"How do you make good decisions?" the young man asked.
"Experience," the banker replied.
The young man thought for a moment, and then inquired, "How do you get experience?"
With a warm smile, aged with wisdom, the older man replied, "Bad decisions!"[6]

192

We grow in discernment in much the same way. We make decisions, and we gain experience as we step out in faith trying to listen to the Holy Spirit. Through experience we learn how to better tune into what God is showing us and how to better interpret the signs He is showing us. If we miss something, we can learn from the mistake and grow. Learning a skill (even one that is a spiritual gift) requires practice and training.

The reality is that when spiritual gifts are used, mistakes are often made. People are human. Paul instructs his readers, "Test everything. Hold on to the good" (1 Thess 5:21). The Bible does not encourage believers to test everything and throw it all out. Too often that is what happens with spiritual gifts. Too often mistakes have led to throwing the baby out with the bath water. Instead of running away from God's gifts He has given His Church to be more effective, Christians should obey this command: "Pursue spiritual gifts, especially that you may prophesy" (1 Cor 14:1). We need spiritual gifts to improve our ability to see better!

When God reveals something, we need discernment to know how that revelation is to be communicated. Just because we "see" something does not mean we are supposed to share everything we see with everyone at any time. We need discernment, and often the gift of wisdom, to know where, when, and how to share revelation that God gives.

Prophecy, in particular, should be judged by the fruit it produces (Matt 7:15ff). Does the word honor Christ and bring glory to Him (John 16:14; 1 Cor 12:3)? Does the word edify, exhort, and comfort (1 Cor 14:3)? God may have us mention something negative, but His purposes are always redemptive. What is the spirit behind the prophecy?

We should also consider the person prophesying. Does his or her teaching agree with Scripture? Does the person emphasize the redemptive work of Christ? Is there any manipulation? Does this person walk in humility? Does the individual's ministry produce humility and the fruit of the Holy Spirit? Are the person's words accurate? The answers to these questions give us discernment about the validity of the prophecy itself.

Another illustration from banking can help us with discernment. When bankers receive training to recognize counterfeit bills, they often learn more about the nuances of real bills than about all the ways a bill can be forged. How does a real bill feel? Where are the watermarks? Are there blue and red threads? When bankers grasp the many details of a real bill, fake ones stand out as being counterfeit. In the same way, the best way to develop discernment is to become deeply familiar with the Holy Spirit and His work. When something happens that does not "fit," we can begin to question its source.

Learning how to discern whether revelation is from God or not is an important component to seeing well. R. T. Kendall gives the acronym PEACE for sharpening our discernment. This acronym outlines a general approach to knowing God's will and whether or not we have truly heard God's voice.

P—Providence. Is the word providential? If God gives a word, it will cohere or align with His providence. In other words, does God open the door, or do we have to knock it down? If we have to pry a door open, it is a fairly good hint we are acting in the flesh.

E—the Enemy. What would your enemy, the devil, want you to do? He comes as a roaring lion and masquerades as an angel of light (2 Cor 11:14, 1 Pet 5:8). The roaring lion comes to intimidate and scare. The "roar" is to make you say, "I'm finished," so you will give in and let him destroy you. Knowing what the devil wants you to do can help you discern what God wants you to do.

A—Authority. What does the Bible say? The Holy Spirit will never lead us to do anything contrary to God's revealed will—the Bible. "How can a young man keep his way pure? By living according to your Word" (Ps 119:9). One way to discern if we are seeing correctly is to compare what we are seeing with what God's Word says.

C—Confidence. Does the impression you have received increase or diminish your confidence? Be honest here. Does the thought of obeying this "word" increase your confidence? If so, that is a good sign.

E—Ease. Are you being true to yourself? Ease is what you feel in your heart of hearts, what you feel deep down inside when you are being true to yourself. God will never lead you to be untrue to yourself. He will never lead you in such a way that you violate your conscience.[7]

Finally, never let your desire for the revelation given by spiritual gifts keep you from passionately spending time in God's Word. As Kendall notes, "Some seem more interested in God's *secret* will than they are in His *revealed* will."[8] God wants us to see spiritual gifts, but they should never overshadow the work of God's clearly revealed Word in our lives. We need both to see well!

How Do You See It?

1. How has God used you in the area of spiritual gifts?

2. What spiritual gifts do you feel God wants you to develop more?

3. What guidance does God's word give us for discernment with spiritual gifts?

STRATEGY #9

KEEP A SABBATH

Remember the Sabbath day, to keep it holy.
Exodus 20:8

The seventh commandment, "Remember the Sabbath day" (Exod 20:8), is another strategy that helps us see better as followers of Christ. To see like God, we need to follow His example of rest. God worked six days in creating the earth. Then on the seventh day, the Sabbath, He modeled for us the importance of rest:

> And on the seventh day God finished his work that he had done, and he rested on the seventh day from all his work that he had done. So, God blessed the seventh day and made it holy, because on it God rested from all his work that he had done in creation (Gen 2:2-3).

God did not rest on the Sabbath because He was tired or needed rest. He rested as an example for us to follow. He rested because He knew humans would need rest. He also rested before the Fall, indicating that from the beginning God's plan has been for sabbath to play an important role in our lives. To gain God's perspective in life, we need to follow God's ways, which includes taking sabbath rest.

To gain God's perspective in life, we need to follow God's ways, which includes taking sabbath rest.

Observing sabbaths gives us perspective that we do not gain in our normal workday schedule. Saying "No" to work brings a disruption that helps us notice things we normally do not see. During sabbath we are involved in different activities than usual. As we alter our routine, we observe things that we normally do not notice. New activities lead to new observations and opportunities for growth.

Depending on the day of the week we observe sabbath, church attendance may or may not be a part of our experience. Observant Jews (and Seventh-day Adventists) strictly observe sabbath on Saturdays and have worship services on the same. Christ followers have historically observed a time of sabbath rest on Sundays, the day of Christ's resurrection. Attending church services on Sunday mornings has long been a tradition of Christ followers and provides great opportunities for growth in spiritual sight.

A key reason for attending services on one's chosen sabbath day is to enhance community as the Body of Christ. We see better together (see Strategy #6). Aside from a church service, though, spending time with other members of the Body of Christ during part of our sabbath time gives opportunities for spiritual growth and service. We do not want to forsake the assembling of ourselves together (Heb 10:25).

For some Christ followers, observing a time of sabbath on Sundays is not always a good option. Some jobs require duty on

Sundays. Christian clergy also have difficulty observing a personal sabbath on Sundays when they are required to work during Sunday worship services. When we observe a sabbath time is not the key issue, but rather our obedience in actually observing sabbath.

To gain the most perspective from times of sabbath, reflection should be a part of our experience. Attending a worship service can be a good opportunity for this. Others may choose to reflect alone. For sabbath to truly function as a sabbath, some space for reflection is necessary. God created the world and then rested, reflecting on His work. Christ followers need rhythmic opportunities to reflect on what God has done, is doing, and wants to do in our lives.

God gives perspective to those who seek it. Sabbath is a unique perspective-gaining opportunity needed by all Christ followers to ascertain God's work and how we are to follow Him in the same. Ronald Heifetz and Marty Linsky talk about the need for perspective in business and life:

> Few practical ideas are more obvious or more critical than the need to get perspective in the midst of action. Any military officer, for example, knows the importance of maintaining the capacity for reflection, even in the 'fog of war.' Great athletes can at once play the game and observe it as a whole—as Walt Whitman described it, 'being both in and out of the game.' Jesuits call it 'contemplation in action.' ... We call this skill 'getting off the dance floor and going to the balcony,' an image that captures the mental activity of stepping back in the midst of action and asking, 'What's really going on here?'[1]

Regularly observing sabbath gives believers opportunities to disengage from life as normal, so that greater perspective can be obtained. God gives us balcony views as we allow Him time and attention.

Throughout history, the Sabbath has helped Israel see their identity as God's people. There is a Jewish saying (by the Ahad Ha'am) that says, "More than the Jewish People have kept Shabbat, Shabbat has kept the Jews."[2] The Sabbath has been a defining marker in the lives of Jews since Israel received the Ten

Commandments. Observance of sabbath rest can help Christ followers see themselves as members of Christ's Body as they use part of their sabbath to be in Christian community and use sabbath time to grow spiritually.

The Sabbath also helped the Jews to see themselves as free because of God's deliverance. They had been slaves in Egypt, but God brought them out as a nation and gave them the Sabbath. No longer were they forced to work seven days a week. No longer were they under the oppression of others. They were a nation free to be God's people. The Sabbath was a reminder of all that God had done for them. In Deuteronomy 5:15, God exhorts Israel: "You shall remember that you were a slave in the land of Egypt, and the Lord your God brought you out from there with a mighty hand and an outstretched arm. Therefore, the Lord your God commanded you to keep the Sabbath day."

Just as the Sabbath helped Israel see themselves as free, Christ followers also see themselves free from sin and the bondage of being defined by their production, work or anything else other than Christ. Gaining freedom from many things requires surrender and focus. Sabbath can give time to reflect on what God has already done in our lives and to surrender in areas still needed.

Abraham Heschel writes that other religions often began by setting apart sacred places, whereas Israel, in the Sabbath, set apart a sacred time, for time is the stuff of life.[3] No matter where Jews live today, they are to observe Sabbath. No matter where Christ followers reside, we too are to observe a day of rest and reflection upon who we are as Christ's people. We can keep sabbath wherever we are located.

Observing a sabbath gives us an opportunity see work in a healthier, more balanced way. Workaholism and slothfulness are both extremes God wants us to avoid. Taking a sabbath helps us see that we are much more than what we do. Sabbath keeping helps us replenish ourselves. Life and people are demanding.

The more we succeed, the more we lead. The more we lead, the more people demand of us. At creation God saw the need for rest. Sabbath is His gift to us.

Sabbath keeping seems to have good medical benefits as well. Years ago, one researcher discovered that in Jewish communities, mortality rates plummet on the Sabbath. Why? The researcher concluded that even the sick and terminally ill rallied for the Sabbath day because it was a chance to be with family and friends.[4] There seems also to be a scientifically based connection between Sabbath-keeping and longer life expectancy.[5] On average, Seventh-day Adventists live ten years longer than the overall North American life expectancy. Ten years! Obeying God may not be a motivating factor for some people, but living longer definitely is. While our chief motivating factor ought to be obeying God, living longer could be an added benefit!

Vince Lombardi is credited with saying, "Fatigue makes cowards of us all."[6] Another way to say that is this: When fatigue walks in, faith walks out! When we are tired, our faith usually wanes. Many zealous preachers have made statements about the importance of giving our all to God. One preacher said, "I'd rather flame out than rust out." The problem with this is that either way, you're out. Once we're out, it doesn't matter much how we got there. Other people have said, "The devil never takes a vacation, so why should we?" This is bad theology. The devil is not supposed to be our example. God is our example, and He rested, commanding us to do the same. If we break God's commandments, we are actually breaking ourselves. Sabbath keeping is no exception. When we fail to keep the Sabbath, we set ourselves up for burnout or loss of focus on God's priorities.

God designed the sabbath for us (Mark 2:27). We miss a gift from Him if we choose to ignore it. Let's follow His example in honoring the Sabbath. We need it for spiritual health and His perspective.

How Do You See It?

1. Has there been a time in your life when a new environment or schedule has helped you gain a new perspective on an important matter?

2. How does sabbath keeping give us perspective?

3. How does sabbath keeping affect our view of work?

STRATEGY #10

AVOID SIN

"Consecrate, then concentrate."[1]
—*motto of Dwight L. Moody*

P art of life in Minnesota is clearing off snow from our car windshields. Fresh-fallen snow does not look dangerous *per se*, but when it covers windshields, it becomes quite hazardous. Anything that impedes clear vision while driving should be avoided. Likewise, anything that impedes our spiritual vision must be removed.

We have emphasized the importance of seeing well so we can live well. It is possible physically to see perfectly well, though, and still not notice important things around us. Sometimes our problem is distraction.

Our attention is valuable. That is one reason why we "pay" it! Our attention represents our time and life itself. We need to be careful to stay focused on what God has for us and avoid distractions. Some distractions are obvious—a second gaze at someone who is not our spouse, a lingering romantic imagination we know is not pure. Sometimes distractions are not as obvious—an extra look at the sports score, another glance at our phone, or a stare at colorful fall trees on the side of the road. Good things can easily distract us from great things God is calling us to do at any given moment. We constantly need God's help to discern what is most important during a given season of our life and to stay focused on priorities.

Not all distractions are sinful, but sin is always distracting. It causes us to fall short of God's plans for us, the glory of God (Rom 3:23). When we pay attention to sin, we start moving away from the greatness God has prepared for us. We also start losing connection with the ONE who can enable us to fulfill the purposes for which we were created.

When we allow ourselves to get distracted by sin, we grieve God and separate ourselves from the fullness of His presence. The Psalmist writes, "If I had cherished sin in my heart, the Lord would not have listened" (Ps 66:18, NIV). Isaiah writes, "Surely the arm of the Lord is not too short to save, nor his ear too dull to hear. But your iniquities have separated you from your God; your sins have hidden his face from you, so that he will not hear" (Isa 59:1-2, NIV).

> ## "Not all distractions are sinful, but sin is always distracting. It causes us to fall short of God's plans for us, the glory of God."
> —*Romans 3:23*

When we sin and are separated from the fullness of God's presence, we lose at least some measure of spiritual perception. Our lenses get muddied. We are not able to fully receive help from God because of our sin. Samson was so blinded by his ongoing lust that he betrayed the secret of his strength. Then he did not even realize his loss of the Lord's presence as he went to fight the Philistines who seized him and gouged out his eyes (Judg 16:1-21).

When we choose sin, we choose thought patterns and values that distract us from God's purposes. We get distracted from what God is saying to us. We stop paying attention to Him.

Not paying attention can be dangerous in many ways ...

A story is told about Dr. William Osler, a famous professor of medicine at Oxford, and a small bottle containing urine that sat upon his desk. Osler was sitting in a classroom full of young, wide-eyed medical students listening to his lecture on the importance of observing details. To emphasize his point, Osler reached down and picked up the bottle of urine. Holding it high, he announced: "This bottle contains a sample for analysis. It's often possible by tasting it to determine the disease from which the patient suffers." Suiting action to words, he dipped a finger into the fluid and then into his mouth, as he continued, "Now I am going to pass the bottle around. Each of you please do exactly as I did. Perhaps we can learn the importance of this technique and diagnose the case." The bottle made its way from row to row as each student gingerly poked his finger in and bravely sampled the contents with a frown. Dr. Osler then retrieved the bottle and startled his students with these words: "Students, now you will understand what I mean when I speak about details. Had you been observant you would have seen that I put my index finger into the bottle but my middle finger into my mouth!"[2] Paying attention often saves us from embarrassing mistakes!

Paying attention also can help us avoid sin. One definition of sin is "missing the mark." We miss the mark a lot when we do not pay attention! As we stay focused on Christ, our lives are far more fruitful, and we stay far from sin.

The writer of Hebrews exhorts us to fix our eyes on Jesus, the Author and the Perfector of our faith. Jesus is our magnificent obsession. He is our Lord. He is our everything! As we focus on Christ, distractions lose their attraction. Sin loses its lure. When we truly encounter Jesus, things on earth grow strangely dim in the light of His glory and grace.

How Do You See It?

1. What can you do to avoid sin and see its danger more clearly?

2. Sometimes sharing a struggle with a fellow believer gives us strength and accountability. Who is someone with whom you can talk when facing sin or temptation?

3. What can you do to focus more on Jesus?

STRATEGY #11

ELIMINATE DISTORTION

"False ideas are the greatest obstacles to the reception of the Gospel."[1]
—*J. Gresham Machen.*

My wife and I used to visit a theme park that had a room with fun-house mirrors. Some helped you quickly "grow taller and thinner," but the distortions of other mirrors were not always as flattering. While the mirrors were good for some laughs, it was also good to be able to walk away from the mirrors knowing we did not look as bad as the curved glass made us appear.

Distortion is unfortunately not limited to fun-house mirrors. Along with distracting us with sin, Satan loves to warp our spiritual vision by convincing us to believe lies. When we believe a lie, we give the enemy power in that area of our lives. We give him control that should not be his. When we allow ourselves to believe falsehood, we give authority to the enemy and fall short of thinking the way

God intends. We miss opportunities for growth and Kingdom impact when we allow ourselves to continue thinking a lie.

When we believe a lie, we give the enemy power in that area of our life. We give him control that should not be his.

To see better, we need to grow in discerning lies and then avoid them at all costs. Lies taint the way we see reality. They influence us to make poor choices.

> Ethiopians share a story about a boy who had a pet lamb. He fed it by hand and played with it every day. When hard times came, he was forced to take his pet lamb to the town market to sell it. Three thieves who heard of the boy's plan plotted to take the lamb from him. Early in the morning the boy rose and put the lamb over his shoulders to carry it to market. As he traveled down the road, the first thief approached him and said, "Why are you carrying that dog on your shoulders?"
>
> The boy laughed, "This is not a dog. It is my pet lamb. I am taking it to market," he said.
>
> After he walked a bit further the second thief crossed his path and said, "What a fine-looking dog you have! Where are you taking it?"
>
> Puzzled, the boy took the lamb off his shoulders and looked carefully at it. "This is not a dog," he said slowly. "It is a lamb, and I am taking it to market."
>
> Shortly before he reached the market the third thief met the boy and said, "Young man, I don't think they will allow you to take your dog into the market."
>
> Completely confused, the boy took the lamb off his shoulders and set it on the ground. "If three different people say this is a dog, then surely it must be a dog," he thought. He tied the lamb to a tree and walked to the market. He never bothered to turn around and see the thieves untying the lamb and going toward their home.[2]

We must reject lies the enemy speaks, no matter how many times we hear them. *Just because a lie is repeated does not make it true.* Lies twist and warp reality. They harm our spiritual vision.

Use Your Primary Lie Detector: God's Word

How do we detect lies the enemy is sowing? If we hear something that conflicts with God's Word, we should be aware that we are hearing a lie. If an idea clashes with the Bible, red flags should start waving! God's Word is the best lie detector—it is our standard for truth.

To discern lies quickly, we must keep ourselves immersed in God's Word, meditating on it throughout our day. The Psalmist pronounces, "Blessed is the man who does not walk in the counsel of the wicked nor stand in the way of sinners nor sits in the seat of scoffers; but his delight is in the law of the Lord, and on his law he meditates day and night" (Ps 1:1-2). (Refer also to Strategy #2.)

We must know the promises of God and His heart toward us. We need regular times in God's Word so that when the enemy brings lies to us, we recognize them as counterfeit sooner than later. We must be on an ongoing discipleship journey in the Word of God!

Jesus said we will know the truth, and the truth will make us free (John 8:32). Just as putting on a pair of glasses with the correct prescription helps our natural eyesight, focusing on God's truth help us see clearly spiritually. Believing a lie is like putting a partial blindfold or patch over one of our eyes. Meditating on God's Word helps us to avoid falling for lies and enables us to see God, ourselves, and our situation clearly.

Use Your Secondary Lie Detector: A Lack of Hope

Another red flag alerting us to lies is the lack of hope we start to feel. When we stop seeing with hope, there is a lie we need to detect and get rid of. Our hope level is a good indicator of whether we are believing truth or lies. When we sense that we are starting to be low on hope, we need to examine what is causing the lack of hope. Most likely we are starting to believe a lie. We need God to help us identify the lie and replace it with Christ's truth.

Our hopelessness about a problem is normally a bigger problem than the problem itself. Christ is always ultimately victorious. Steve Backlund shares, "There are no hopeless circumstances, only hopeless people."[3] Once someone gets true hope, the circumstance cannot stay the same. When we have hope, we see the world differently.

Martin Luther said, "Everything that is done in this world is by hope."[4] When we believe lies and lose our hope, there is no action. If we believe that God will not provide a job, we will not look for one. If we believe a relationship cannot be improved, we will not work on it. If we believe we cannot pass a test, we do not study. It has been said, "We can live forty days without food, eight days without water, four minutes without air, but only a few seconds without hope."[5] Hope is essential for the believer.

When we start to lose hope, we must recognize the lies we are starting to believe and take action.

When we begin to lose hope, we must recognize the lies we are starting to believe and take action. Francis Frangipane warns us that "any system of thinking that does not have hope, which feels hopeless, is a stronghold which must be pulled down."[6] We must do the hard work of identifying hidden strongholds of our hearts where hope does not glisten and detecting the hidden lies. This is not always easy, but God will help us if we ask.

Rooting out lies can also be hard because people may ridicule our efforts. People may accuse us of wearing rose-colored glasses, of not viewing "the reality" of our circumstances. Abraham undoubtedly wrestled with the reality of his and Sarah's old age, yet against all hope, in hope he believed that he would become the father of many nations (Rom 4:18). He refused to believe the lie of being too old for God to provide a son. Abraham held onto the hope that what God had promised was true. He believed that God would work in spite of his circumstances. Isaac's birth proved God true and the enemy a liar.

Stopping Lies

Soon after arriving in India, my wife and I were in language school learning Hindi. We studied a lot and were constantly trying to find ways in our community to use and practice the Hindi we were learning. Having both served in ministry with children in the United States, we were naturally drawn to India's children and decided to begin a children's club in our neighborhood. We would be able to practice our Hindi, and the children would be introduced to Jesus and the Bible—a win/win!

One day after teaching the Easter story, we asked the children questions to review and check their comprehension. One of our questions was, "Did Jesus stay in the tomb?" My wife and I were both expecting the answer of *"Nahin!"* ("No!") or *"Galath!"* ("False!")—the words the kids had used for previous negative responses—but to our surprise, three kids SCREAMED out the word *"Jhoot!"* which means, "LIE!"

"Lie" was not the answer we were expecting, but it was even more true than "No!" or "False!" Their answer emphasized how the enemy constantly sows lies about Christ's death and resurrection. Satan relentlessly tries to get the world to believe that Jesus did not really rise from the dead. He further spreads any other falsehood he thinks he can get us to believe. Those three Indian children shouted out the right response to the enemy's ploy: "LIE!"

Today the father of lies continues to whisper untruths and distortions of the truth. He speaks lies constantly: "You are not going to make it." "You do not measure up." "You have no value." "You're not going to have enough money to pay your bills." And perhaps the most insidious lie of all is "God does not love you. He does not care about you or your situation."

To keep clear vision, we must fight against the lies the enemy sends. In 2 Corinthians Paul exhorts us to take every thought captive to the obedience of Christ (2 Cor 10:5). We must reject any thought that is not from God as it will only serve to divert us from the destiny and purpose God has for us. Followers of Christ cannot afford to have any thought in our heads that is not in God's.

How Do You See It?

1. What are two lie detectors we can use to detect lies?

2. What are some common lies the enemy tries to sow in your thoughts?

3. What are biblical responses you can use to defeat the lies you mentioned in answer to question #2?

STRATEGY #12

OBEY WHAT GOD HAS ALREADY REVEALED

"Go as far as you can see; when you get there, you will be able to see further." [1]
—*Thomas Carlyle*

Our family enjoys escape rooms. We do not always escape, but the challenge is fun, and the teamwork of solving puzzles together is a great bonding experience. There is a thrill when we do manage to solve the puzzles and get out of the room before we "die" or fail in our quest.

Most of the time to succeed in escape rooms, you need to solve riddles or find clues that lead to other clues. If you fail to follow the directions of the clues you find, then you generally fail to get more clues. In one sense, following through the known is key to moving forward.

In our walk with God, if we want to see more, we normally need to follow or obey what we already know to be true. Jesus emphasizes the importance of obedience and stewardship in the parable of the talents:

> For it will be like a man going on a journey, who called his servants and entrusted to them his property. To one he gave five talents, to another two, to another one, to each according to his ability. Then he went away. He who had received the five talents went at once and traded with them, and he made five talents more. So also he who had the two talents made two talents more. But he who had received the one talent went and dug in the ground and hid his master's money. Now after a long time the master of those servants came and settled accounts with them. And he who had received the five talents came forward, bringing five talents more, saying, "Master, you delivered to me five talents; here, I have made five talents more." His master said to him, "Well done, good and faithful servant. You have been faithful over a little; I will set you over much. Enter into the joy of your master." And he also who had the two talents came forward, saying, "Master, you delivered to me two talents; here, I have made two talents more." His master said to him, "Well done, good and faithful servant. You have been faithful over a little; I will set you over much. Enter into the joy of your master." He also who had received the one talent came forward, saying, "Master, I knew you to be a hard man, reaping where you did not sow, and gathering where you scattered no seed, so I was afraid, and I went and hid your talent in the ground. Here, you have what is yours." But his master answered him, "You wicked and slothful servant! You knew that I reap where I have not sown and gather where I scattered no seed? Then you ought to have invested my money with the bankers, and at my coming I should have received what was my own with interest. So, take the talent from him and give it to him who has the ten talents. For to everyone who has will more be given, and he will have an abundance. But from the one who has not, even what he has will be taken away" (Matt 25:14-29).

God rewards those who are faithful with the talents and revelation they have been given. He rewards obedience, blessing those who follow His ways. One of the ways God blesses is by giving improved spiritual insight; greater revelation is the reward for obedience to previously given revelation.

David was a man to whom God revealed himself greatly. In Acts 13:22, David is also called a man after God's heart. No other person in Scripture is referenced this way or given this honor. What was the key to David's being a person after God's heart? Acts 13:22 goes on to say, "He [David] will do everything I want him to do." David's obedience to God connected him to God in a special way. David's obedience helped him see God's heart like few other people.

Unfortunately, Solomon, David's son and heir to the throne of Israel, did not continue in obedience to God. Solomon started well. In fact, 1 Kings 11:9 notes that God even appeared to Solomon, not just once, but twice (1 Kgs 3:5-14, 9:2). With such revelation came great responsibility. Sadly, Solomon's heart turned away from God, and God became angry with him. Solomon squandered all God had revealed to him.

If we do not obey God's revelation, we suffer consequences. If we continue in disobedience, at some point God stops giving revelation and our hearts are in danger of being darkened. Paul warns in Romans 1:21, "For although they knew God, they did not honor him as God or give thanks to him, but they became futile in their thinking, and their foolish hearts were darkened." When we turn away from God's revelation, our hearts become dark and we become blind.

To see more in the Kingdom, we must be responsibly obedient to what God has already given. God normally gives us enough revelation to lead us to the next step He wants us to take. If we hesitate to obey Him in taking the next step, then we may not receive more revelation. Our sight may be limited by our lack of obedience.

When we drive a car at night on a dark road, the car's headlights enable us to see a certain distance in front of us. As we drive the car forward, we are actually able to see further as the car's headlights continue to shine and give illumination further down the road than what we could see before. If we park the car, however, we do not continue to see more and more area lit up in front of us. It is only by moving forward that we see more. Likewise, it is only by moving forward in obedience to what we know God wants us to do that He shows us even more revelation for our next steps.

"You will know as much of God, and only as much of God, as you are willing to put into practice."
—*Eric Liddell*

When we live a lifestyle of repeated obedience to God, He rewards us. One of the best ways God rewards us is with more revelation, with an even greater ability to see and understand. As we see and understand more, then we are able to obey more, then see and understand even more, and on it goes. As Scottish Olympic runner and missionary Eric Liddell said, "You will know as much of God, and only as much of God, as you are willing to put into practice."[2]

How Do You See It?

1. Are you obeying God in what He has shown you to do? Is there an area where you need to step up your obedience?

2. When you disobey God, what is usually the reason? Fear? Rebellion? Addiction? Insecurity?

3. What is one way God rewards us when we obey Him?

STRATEGY #13

RENEW AND EXPAND YOUR THINKING

"Do not conform any longer to the pattern of this world, but be transformed by the renewing of your mind. Then you will be able to test and approve what God's will is—his good, pleasing and perfect will."
Romans 12:2, NIV

Just as our natural eyesight's ability is connected with our brain, our spiritual ability to see is connected with our mind. Having a renewed mind is critical to seeing as Christ sees and correctly interpreting what we see. Even more than thinking analytically, Christ followers should pursue thinking like Christ. Learning independence and free thinking are good pursuits, but no one thinks and sees better than God does. No amount of education can substitute for a renewed mind. Only God can see all of reality. Only He has the perspective we need most. Any perspective less than God's will be imperfect at best. Renewing our minds must be a priority so we think more and more like Christ and see the world more and more the way He does.

It was at Golgotha, the place of the skull, that the devil unleashed his greatest attack on Christ. Praise God! Christ defeated him there. Isn't it interesting that our minds, often associated with our skulls, are the place where the devil attacks us most? Paul writes,

> For though we walk in the flesh, we are not waging war according to the flesh. For the weapons of our warfare are not of the flesh but have divine power to destroy strong-holds. We destroy arguments and every lofty opinion raised against the knowledge of God, and take every thought captive to obey Christ (2 Cor 10:3-5).

Having a mind like Christ, the ultimate Victor, equips us to defeat the devil too!

Repentance, the cry of John the Baptist when preparing for Christ's arrival, is part of the process of our mind being renewed. The word "repentance" in Greek is *metanoia*, which means changing one's mind or the way one thinks. Metamorphosis is another English word that gives a picture of what *meta* means. A worm metamorphosizes into a butterfly. Major change happens to the worm for this transformation to occur, and major change is needed for our thinking. Our thinking must be changed so it aligns with God's thinking. Repentance is the first step.

How often should we repent? Whenever our thoughts are not like God's!

How often should we repent? Whenever our thoughts are not like God's! We constantly need God to help us see areas in our lives where we need to have His view instead of ours, where our thoughts do not line up with Scripture. This discipleship process is painfully hard and long. We must have God's strength and endurance to keep aligning our thoughts with His.

God's Word and discernment must remain a part of the process of renewing our minds. As we discussed in Strategy #2, God's Word is the foundation of a biblical worldview. It is also the basis for a renewed mind. We must allow God's Word, and not merely our feelings, experiences, and hurts, to shape the way we see. When our feelings, experiences, or hurts lead us to wrong thoughts, we need to repent.

In Deuteronomy God instructed Israel's kings to prioritize His Word by writing out the Word of God:

> And when he sits on the throne of his kingdom, he shall write for himself in a book a copy of this law, approved by the Levitical priests. And it shall be with him, and he shall read in it all the days of his life, that he may learn to fear the Lord his God by keeping all the words of this law and these statutes, and doing them, that his heart may not be lifted up above his brothers, and that he may not turn aside from the commandment, either to the right hand or to the left, so that he may continue long in his kingdom, he and his children, in Israel (vv. 18-20).

God's purpose in having the king write out the Law by hand was to help the king have a renewed mind, so he could better see what actions and decisions he should take. God's Word was a tool to guide the king in how he saw his kingdom and responsibilities. We ought to consider writing out God's Word by hand ourselves, but even if we do not actually write it out with our hands, we can type or at least cut and paste! We need to take time to meditate upon God's Law. Finding ways to pray over and reflect on God's Word is critical for a renewed mind. We want God's Word to be imprinted on our lives!

As we gain a renewed mind, here are some of the ways our vision improves:

1. We see our limitations and become more dependent on God. We realize that our ability to make lasting impact is small, but God can do much through us.

2. We look to God's Word for regular realignments in our thinking.

3. We are concerned not just about the here and now, but also about eternity.

4. We are more humble and thankful, realizing we have received many benefits we do not deserve.

5. We see ourselves as part of Christ's Body, and we honor the perspectives of others who have valuable insights from their places in the body.

6. We use our spiritual gifts, understanding God's abilities are way more than ours.

7. We take time to reflect and rest, allowing God to reveal Himself to us in new environments.

8. We see the danger of sin and avoid it all cost.

9. We are passionate to obey what God has revealed, in part because we want Him to reveal even more.

10. We are passionate about thinking the way God thinks!

11. We have more hope because we readily recognize lies better. Instead of meditating on the enemy's twisted thoughts, we reject them. We see our circumstances and realize, "God will see us through! God will meet our needs!"

12. The impossible looks reasonable when our mind is renewed. When God says He's going to do something we have never experienced before, we believe it will happen. We believe all things are possible with God!

13. We live in peace because our thoughts are positive. We do not entertain negative speculations. What could that look like? If your spouse comes home late from work,

where does your mind go? If your mind is renewed, even your speculations are hopeful. So, you'd think, "Maybe the boss kept my spouse late to give him/her a promotion," instead of, "Maybe he/she was in a wreck."

Often the main limitation for God is between our ears. A renewed mind actually helps us see better. Rather than our brain stopping God's work in our lives, a renewed mind helps us see things correctly and propels us forward. May God renew our minds!

Increase Your Learning

Another way we increase our ability to see better is to pursue not only a renewed mind but also an expanded mind. If we want to see more, we need to learn more. We need to know more. This suggestion may not seem "spiritual," but it is very true: If you want to see better in any area of life, learn more about that area. An art critic and a novice look at the same painting and see totally different things. The art critic has spent years learning about principles related to art and can appreciate many nuances that an untrained person cannot. Astronomers without the aid of a telescope may often see more than typical people looking at the stars with a telescope. Why? Astronomers know stars. They have a huge frame of reference to use when examining particular parts of the universe.

If you want to see better in any area of life, learn more about that area.

Not long ago we went with our youngest daughter to the dental specialties department at the Mayo Clinic. At her appointment, the doctors showed us an X-ray of my daughter's wisdom teeth that needed extracting. I could look at the X-ray and tell I was looking at teeth. I even could discern which teeth were likely the wisdom teeth and which ones were molars and incisors. My dad was a dentist, so I grew up learning a little about dentistry. However, my knowledge of dental X-rays is still pretty much limited to recognizing I am looking at teeth. When general dentists look at an oral X-ray, they see a lot more than I do. When specialty dentists at Mayo Clinic look at an X-ray, they see even more than a general dentist. The more we learn, the more details we see.

Knowing more often provides us with more interests to fill in our lives. This in turn creates new levels of curiosity. Curiosity is a great motivator for paying more attention and seeing more. The more we know, the more we understand the need to learn and see more.

Research, study, and learn from others who have insight in the fields and subjects God has placed on your heart. Learning is one of the ways we sharpen our abilities to see not only what others have seen, but new things God wants to reveal. By studying and learning we can prepare ourselves both naturally and supernaturally to see better.

Ralph Waldo Emerson said, "People see only what they are prepared to see."[1] This is at least partially true. People do see things better when they have been prepared to see versus when they are unprepared. Learning helps us to be better prepared to see the many things God wants to show us!

How Do You See It?

1. What are some ways your vision improves as you gain a renewed mind?

2. How does learning more about an area of life help you to see more in that area and in all of life?

3. What does God want you to learn more about so that you can see even more?

STRATEGY #14

FOCUS ON GOD'S GREATNESS

"He performs wonders that cannot be fathomed,
miracles that cannot be counted."
Job 5:9 NIV

In Numbers 13 the Lord told Moses, "Send men to spy out the land of Canaan, which I am giving to the people of Israel. From each tribe of their fathers you shall send a man, every one a chief among them" (Num 13:1-2). These men were to spy out the Promised Land and bring back a report on how to conquer the land. The spies went out and were stunned at the goodness of the land. After forty days they returned with fruit from the land and a report of the land being full of milk and honey. The Israelites were amazed at the samples of fruit the spies brought back and the reports of how wonderful the land was. However, ten of the spies saw the challenges of the new land as being too great. They began to talk about how powerful the inhabitants of the land were and their fortified cities. The ten spies emphasized how difficult it would be to take the land, describing the inhabitants as giants. The ten shared how they felt like grasshoppers and that they seemed like grasshoppers to the inhabitants of the land (Num 13:33). The ten spies urged Israel to not go up and take the land God had given them. (By the way, have you ever wondered how they knew how the inhabitants saw them?)

Joshua and Caleb were the two spies who saw things differently. They urged Israel not to rebel against God. God had promised Israel the land, so they urged, "Do not fear the people of the land ... their protection is removed from them, and the Lord is with us; do not fear them" (Num 14:9). Unfortunately, Israel's response was to side with the ten spies and to threaten Joshua and Caleb with stoning.

God was not impressed with the way the ten spies saw the challenges and gave their report; neither was He impressed with the Israelites' response. God is never impressed when we see our obstacles as being bigger than Him. God had sent the leaders from Israel on a mission to spy out (see) the land and bring back information on how to conquer, not on how to retreat. God who had brought them all the way from Egypt—including across a dry Red Sea bed—had promised Israel the land, but Israel's leaders allowed the perceived challenges of the Promised Land to intimidate them.

God is never impressed when we see our obstacles as being bigger than Him.

In *The Knowledge of the Holy*, A. W. Tozer writes about the importance of our view of God. He notes, "A low view of God is the cause of a hundred lesser evils everywhere among us."[1] We need a high view of God. We need to make sure that we grasp more and more how powerful and awesome He is. Our focus must be on His greatness. Our attention must be riveted on God and what He is doing. As the Psalmist writes, "O magnify the Lord with me" (Ps 34:3). We need to magnify God. God must become bigger in our view. Our focus should never be on the difficulty of what God has called us to do, but on the ONE who has commissioned us. The problems we see in life are real, but God is more real. As Creator, God preceded everything on this planet. He knows far more about our problems than we do.

When printing pictures from a digital file, the size of the file limits how big we can print a picture. If we do not have a file with enough pixels, the picture will print grainy or distorted. Here is some good news: While we are limited in how much we can enlarge printed digital photos, God is not limited by megabytes or pixels in any way or form. We can enlarge a picture of God as big as this planet and still have way more room. We cannot over-exaggerate how big or powerful God is! He is way bigger and more powerful than our minds are capable of grasping.

"A low view of God is the cause of a hundred lesser evils everywhere among us."
–A. W. Tozer

Whatever the size of the problem we see, God is bigger. Whatever the mountain, God is greater. We need to stop telling God how big our mountains are and start telling our mountains how big and powerful our God is. Yes, mountains are real, but we serve a God who can do the impossible. "Not by might, nor by power, but by My Spirit, spirit says the Lord of hosts!" (Zech 4:6). Stop magnifying the problem and start magnifying God.

How is never a problem for God. It is usually a big problem for us, but how is God's specialty. What God originates, He orchestrates. Think back for a minute. Can you remember one biblical story in which the responsibility of figuring out how a divine vision would be fulfilled fell to the man or woman to whom God gave the vision? Did Moses have to come up with a way to get the Israelites out of Egypt? Across the Red Sea? Through the desert? Was it David's responsibility to figure out how to get Saul out of the way so he could ascend the throne of Israel? When Jesus told the apostles to feed the 5,000, were they responsible for figuring out how to make five loaves and two fish go that far? No. In every situation, God orchestrated events in such a way that those involved recognized the hand of God. In the Bible ordinary men and women just did what they knew to do while never losing sight of the vision God had birthed in their hearts. God took care of the how!

Abram had longed for a son with his wife, Sarah, for years. Nothing happened. There were no tests back then to determine the cause. We can guess Sarah had fertility problems because her maid, Hagar, conceived after Sarah sent Abram to sleep with her. There was no science to comfort Abram and Sarah with the possibility of a way to have a son. Circumstances disappointed them over and over. Yet Abram had courage because he saw the future: God had promised Abram he would have a son (Gen 17:16). When Abram was ninety-nine years old, God even gave him a new name, "Abraham," which meant "Father of many nations." Abram believed the promise and accepted his new name, "Abraham." For a full year before Isaac was born, Abraham explained to people, "My name is no longer Abram. My name is 'Abraham,' that is, I am the 'Father of many nations.'" People must have responded, "Father of many nations? Abraham, you are crazy! You are ninety-nine years old, and you have no children with Sarah, not even a daughter." Yet for one full year Abraham spoke in faith, and then after Abraham had turned one hundred years old, Isaac was born!

During the waiting time Abraham faced the facts. He was not out of touch with reality. Yet, Hebrews says Abraham was fully persuaded that God had the power to deliver on His promises. Abraham was able to see his future life with a son, and he believed God to see it come to pass. May we, like Abraham, be known for seeing a big God even when faced with seemingly impossible circumstances. May we acknowledge God's ability to work things together for good, even while in chaos. May we see with eyes of faith no matter the land God calls us to spy out!

How Do You See It?

1. How does a high view of God increase your ability to see clearly?

2. How has God shown himself to be great in your life or in a friend's life? What is an example of Him solving a problem in a way you had not anticipated?

3. What are some Scriptures or biblical stories you can meditate on that emphasize God's greatness?

STRATEGY #15

DON'T LET UNCERTAINTY CRIPPLE YOU

*"Faith is like radar which sees through the
fog the reality of things at a distance that
the human eye cannot see."[1]*
—Corrie ten Boom

In January, the fog in North India can be paralyzing. Some mornings one cannot see more than ten yards away. This makes driving extremely hazardous. I have many friends who have been badly hurt due to accidents caused by fog on the roads. Landing an airplane can be even more dangerous. Flight cancellations and long train delays are commonplace in heavy North Indian fog. The fog is dangerous because of what it hides. One never knows for sure what is ahead—what animals, vehicles, or obstacles stand in your vehicle's path. In the fog, otherwise innocuous obstacles become treacherous when seen too late.

Fog is perhaps most dangerous, though, because it causes us to doubt what we know to be true. Many mornings I looked out our North Indian apartment window and could not see a single building next to ours. I knew there were buildings just fifteen to twenty yards away. I had seen them many times. I had visited friends who lived in them. Yet, on some mornings, all I could see was fog! Did I stop believing that buildings were next door to me? No. Yet sometimes in life the fog of circumstances can tempt us to doubt God and His work in our lives. As Corrie ten Boom said, "Faith is like radar which sees through the fog the reality of things at a distance that the human eye cannot see."[2]

Seeing through the Fog

As we go through life, we may feel as though we are walking through fog. Often, we do not understand what is happening all around us. Circumstances occur that we cannot explain. We sometimes feel alone. We sometimes feel as if no one cares. We do not see how we are going to make it through the challenges we are facing. Fog!

Florence Chadwick was the first woman to ever swim the English Channel in both directions, from England to France, and then from France to England. In 1952, she attempted to swim from Catalina Island in the Pacific Ocean to the shore of California—a trip of twenty-six miles. As she swam, boats surrounded her and people watched for sharks; everyone wanted to witness this historic event. Suddenly, a fog rolled in, and she could no longer see the shoreline. She stopped a half mile short of her destination because she did not know how much farther she had to go.

Two months later, Florence tried again. Again, a fog set in, but this time Florence kept going until she walked onto the shore of California. When later asked how she did it, Florence said, "This time I kept a vision in my mind of the shoreline. I didn't know exactly where it was, but when the fog set in, I kept seeing the shoreline in my mind."[3] During both attempts to swim from Catalina Island to the shore of California, Florence could not see the shoreline, but she knew it was there. During the second attempt, Florence held onto the hope of reaching the beach as she continued with her strokes. She pictured the shoreline in her mind. She did not give up.

How we view things determines what we do. It impacts our level of hope. It impacts our ability to sustain forward motion in the midst of difficult times. Florence initially lost hope when she could not see the shore. Quite often we, too, lose hope and motivation when we cannot see the finish.

When fog surrounds us, God wants to give us faith to see Him and faith to take the next step of obedience. As Martin Luther King, Jr. challenges, "Faith is taking the first step when you don't see the whole staircase."[4] We long to see as far ahead as possible, certainly the next several steps ahead, yet life often does not grant us that luxury. In those times of intense fog, we can be confident of God's presence and goodness. We can trust God's leading for the next step.

"Faith is taking the first step when you don't see the whole staircase."
—Martin Luther King, Jr.

In the midst of fog God wants to assure us that He is the same yesterday, today, and forever (Heb 13:8). Just because we cannot see clearly does not mean that God is not working in us and in our circumstances. As the song "Waymaker" says: "Even when I can't see it, You're working; even when I can't feel it,

You're working. You never stop. You never stop working."[5] While in fog, keep believing what God made very clear to you during clear skies! According to America's Bureau of Standards, a dense fog covering seven city blocks to a depth of one hundred feet contains less than one glass of water. All of that fog, if it could be condensed into water, would not quite fill a drinking glass.[6] Compare this to the things we often worry about. Like fog, our worries can thoroughly block our vision of God's promises, but the fact is, they have little substance to them. Most of the things we worry about never happen. Yet too often we let worry keep us from seeing hope in God.

Stripping Uncertainty of Its Power

The African impala can jump to a height of over ten feet and cover a distance of more than fifty feet. Yet these magnificent creatures can be kept in an enclosure in any zoo with only a three-foot wall. Why? The impalas will not jump if they cannot see where their feet will land.[7]

Too many humans are also trapped by their inability to see what is next. Too many are unwilling to take risks because the outcome is not visible. Too often we let current, visible circumstances keep us from taking actions that will lead us to better circumstances. Sometimes, no matter what we do, we still do not see well. Sometimes we have to deal with uncertainty. Sometimes we have to take steps when clarity is not to be found.

"Faith is taking the first step before God reveals the second step."
—Mark Batterson

Groups of animals have different names based on their species. Groups of cattle are called herds. Birds are called flocks and fish are schools. A group of lions is a pride, a group of buzzards is a committee, and a group of rhinos is called a crash. "Crash" fits a group of rhinos well. Rhinos can run about thirty miles per hour. That is pretty fast! Olympic gold-medalist Usain Bolt's top speed is about twenty-eight miles per hour![8] Unfortunately, rhinos have terrible eyesight. They can only see about thirty feet in front of themselves. So, they are running thirty miles an hour with no idea what is ahead at thirty-one feet! You would think rhinos would be hesitant animals because they cannot see very far, but they are not. (Maybe that is why God gave rhinos a big horn on the front of their head!)

We can learn from a rhino's willingness to move into uncertainty. Sometimes we have to move into places we cannot see well. Mark Batterson shares, "Faith is taking the first step before God reveals the second step."[9]

> When John Kavanaugh went to work for three months at "the house of the dying" in Kolkata, he was seeking a clear answer for how best to spend the rest of his life. During his first morning at the home, he met Mother Teresa. She asked him, "And what can I do for you?"
>
> Kavanaugh asked her to pray for him. "What do you want me to pray for?" she asked.
>
> John then voiced the request that he had carried thousands of miles from the United States: "Pray that I have clarity."
>
> Mother Theresa replied firmly, "No, I will not do that."
>
> When John asked her why, she said, "Clarity is the last thing you are clinging to and must let go of."
>
> When John commented that she always seemed to have the clarity he longed for, she laughed and replied, "I have never had clarity; what I have always had is trust. So, I will pray that you trust God."[10]

Fog is common as we walk through life, yet fog also gives us the opportunity to demonstrate our faith and trust in Christ. When we get to heaven, we will not need faith because everything will be clear. We get to please God now through our faith as we demonstrate our trust in Him when we cannot see as well as we would like to see. May God help us take steps of faith and obedience even when there is a blanket of fog.

How Do You See It?

1. How does uncertainty or not being able to see what is next impact your obedience to God?

2. How does uncertainty or fog impact your attitude?

3. What Scriptures can encourage your faith in times of uncertainty?

Conclusion

A couple of years ago I went online and ordered replacement windshield wipers for my family's car. I had never ordered wipers online before, and it had been a long while since I had replaced a pair of wipers. So, I was somewhat proud of myself when I successfully swapped out the old blades with a new pair.

Soon, though, my satisfaction turned to frustration. While the new blades worked better than the old ones, there were still streaks left on the windshield with the new blades. It was still hard to see, especially during heavy rain.

I had also been wondering about the neon yellow color of the new blades. Neon yellow seemed trendy, but also odd. I figured I'd missed something in the online advertising.

Then one day while I was driving in the rain, the yellow strip on one wiper began to come loose from the rest of the wiper. Concerned, I stopped the car and examined the blades more closely. The yellow part of the wiper was not a part of the wiper at all! It was a packaging cover over the actual blades! I felt stupid and elated at the same time—stupid for not figuring out sooner that the yellow covers were supposed to be removed and elated that finally we had wipers that genuinely worked. We now could see so much better through our windshield!

Fortunately, we did not have any accidents while driving with covered windshield wipers, but poor visibility did cause frustration and likely put us in some danger. Seeing through a partially clear window is nowhere near as safe as seeing through a totally clear one. Over the course of time, the risk of unclear spots presents even more danger.

In life, we need to see as clearly as we can. The way we see greatly impacts our decisions. Even small distortions or blind spots hurt our ability to grasp reality and make good decisions.

Our physical senses can only grasp a small fraction of what is needed to thrive in eternity. Humanly, we can only see one small part of the elephant at a time. Yet God can see all of reality, and He wants to give us His vision. We need God's Word, the Holy Spirit, and spiritual gifts to help us see both spiritual and natural realities with proper perspective.

Daily, our view determines what we do! Then, what we do impacts the quality and outcomes of our lives. At the end, when we stand before God and our lives are tested, will our work be revealed as precious stones or as wood, hay, and straw? (1 Cor 3:12-13). May God help us see reality the way He does, so our lives may have the impact that God has called them to have for His glory!

About the Author

Nick Robertson serves as the director of the Antioch Initiative, a partnership between Assemblies of God World Missions and North Central University focused on the unreached of the world. Prior to serving with the Antioch Initiative, Nick served in Asia for close to twenty years. Nick is grateful for the courageous lives of many Asian Christian leaders and for the privilege of learning much from them.

Endnotes

Introduction

1. John Godfrey Saxe, "The Blind Men and the Elephant," 1873, Commonlit, accessed September 21, 2020, https://www.commonlit.org/texts/the-blind-men-and-the-elephant.

2. All Scripture quotations, unless otherwise noted, are from the ESV.

3. Please compare Matthew 6:22-23 with Luke 11:34, which says, "Your eye is the lamp of your body. When your eye is healthy your whole body is full of light, but when it its bad, your body is full of darkness."

Chapter 2: Seeing through a Different Lens

1. W. Gary Phillips, William E. Brown, and John Stonestreet, *Making Sense of Your World: A Biblical Worldview* (Salem, WI: Sheffield Publishing Company, 2007), 4, Kindle.

2. Jean Johnson, *We Are Not the Hero* (Sisters, OR: Deep River Books), loc. 338-352, Kindle.

3. James W. Sire, *The Universe Next Door: A Basic Worldview Catalog* (Downers Grove, IL: InterVarsity Press, 2009), chap. 1, Kindle.

4. James Anderson, *What's Your Worldview?* (Wheaton: Crossway, 2014), Introduction, Kindle.

5. Phillips, Brown, and Stonestreet, *Making Sense of Your World*, chap. 3.

Chapter 3: Do You Have the Right Prescription?

1. Keith Green, *"All Roads Lead…,"* AZ Quotes, accessed May 30, 2021, https://www.azquotes.com/quote/581847.

2. Tawa J. Anderson, *An Introduction to Christian Worldview* (Downers Grove, IL: InterVarsity Press), chap. 1, Kindle.

3. C. S. Lewis, *God in the Dock* (Grand Rapids, MI: Eerdmans,1970), 110.

4. "Motivating Albert Einstein Quotes," Life Falcon, accessed October 14, 2020, https://lifefalcon.com/all-einstein-quote-simple-explanation/.

Chapter 4: Everybody's Got Faith

1. Mary Poplin, Is Reality Secular?: Testing the Assumptions of Four Global Worldviews (Downers Grove, IL:InterVarsity Press, 2014), 30, Kindle.

2. John Bisagno, quoted in John Maxwell, *Today Matters* (New York: Time Warner, 2004), 205.

3. Allen Tennison, personal correspondence with the author, January 26, 2021.

4. Phillip Johnson, quoted in *I Don't Have Enough Faith to Be an Atheist* (Wheaton: Crossway), 17, Kindle.

Chapter 5: The God Question

1. Ronald Nash, "The Problem of Evil," in *To Everyone an Answer: A Case for the Christian Worldview*, ed. Francis J. Beckwith, William Lane Craig, and J. P. Moreland (Downers Grove, IL: InterVarsity Press, 2004), 248, Kindle.

2. Mortimer Adler, *The Synopticon: An Index to the Great Ideas*, vol. 1 of *The Great Books of the Western World* (Chicago: Britannica, 2005), 433.

3. Tim Keller, "Knowing God," October 10, 2004, Player FM, accessed November 2, 2020, http://player.fm/series/timothy-keller-sermons-podcast-by-gospel-in-life-83408/knowing-god, 8, quoted in Richard E. Simmons III, *Reflections on the Existence of God: A Series of Essays* (Birmingham: The Center for Executive Leadership), chap. 1, Kindle.

4. Ibid.

5. Simmons, *Reflections on the Existence of God*, chap. 1, Kindle.

Chapter 6: What is God Like?

1. A. W. Tozer, *The Knowledge of the Holy* (New Delhi: General Press, 2019), loc. 137, Kindle.

2. Jenn Johnson, Jason Ingram, Ben Fielding, Ed Cash, and Brian Johnson, "Goodness of God," Bethel Music, accessed June 4, 2021, https://bethelmusic.com/chords-and-lyrics/goodness-of-god/.

Chapter 7: Is God Against Sex?

1. Kylie is a friend, whose name has been changed to protect privacy.

2. Joe McIlhaney and Freda McKissic Bush, *Hooked*: New Science on How Casual Sex is Affecting our Children (Chicago: Northfield Publishing, 2008), 129, quoted in Josh McDowell, *Evidence That Demands a Verdict* (Nashville: Thomas Nelson, 2017), liii, Kindle.

3. Ibid.

4. Nancy Pearcey, *Love Thy Body* (Grand Rapids, MI: Baker Publishing Group, 2108), 186, Kindle.

Chapter 8: Does God Care about Suffering?

1. C. S. Lewis, *Mere Christianity* (New York: Harper Collins, 2001), 38.

2. Tim Keller, *The Reason for God* (New York: Penguin Group, 2008), 23.

3. Frank Turek, *I Don't Have Enough Faith to Be an Atheist* (Wheaton: Crossway, 2004), 389, Kindle.

Chapter 9: What about Hell?

1. Lewis, *Problem of Pain*, 130.

2. Matthew 5:22, 29-30; 7:13, 23; 8:12; 10:28; 13:42, 50; 18:8-9; 22:13; 23:15, 33; 24:51; 25:30, 46.

3. "If your right eye causes you to sin, gouge it out and throw it away. It is better for you to lose one part of your body than for your whole body to be thrown into hell. And if your right hand causes you to sin, cut it off and throw it away. It is better for you to lose one part of your body than for your whole body to go into hell" (Matt 5:29-30, NIV).
    "Do not be afraid of those who kill the body but cannot kill the soul. Rather, be afraid of the One who can destroy both soul and body in hell" (Matt 10:28, NIV).

    "And if your eye causes you to sin, gouge it out and throw it away. It is better for you to enter life with one eye than to have two eyes and be thrown into the fire of hell" (Matt 18:9, NIV).

    "If your hand causes you to sin, cut it off. It is better for you to enter life maimed than with two hands to go into hell, where the fire never goes out. And if your foot causes you to sin, cut it off. It is better for you to enter life crippled than to have two feet and be thrown into hell. And if your eye causes you to sin, pluck it out. It is better for you to enter the kingdom of God with one eye than to have two eyes and be thrown into hell (Mark 9:43-47, NIV).

    "What good will it be for someone to gain the whole world, yet forfeit their soul? Or what can anyone give in exchange for their soul? (Matt 16:26, NIV). (The strong implication from Jesus' teaching is that nothing we can gain in this life is worth the price of forfeiting our soul and being separate from God for eternity.)

4. C. S. Lewis, *The Problem of Pain* (New York: Harper Collins, 1996), 122.

5. C. S. Lewis, *The Screwtape Letters* (New York: HarperCollins, 2001), 39.

6. Lewis, *Problem of Pain*, 130.

7. C. S. Lewis, *The Great Divorce* (New York: HarperCollins, 2001), 75.

8. Lewis, *Problem of Pain*, 130.

9. Keller, *The Reason for God*, 76-77.

Chapter 10: The Better We See Him, the More We Love Him

1. Pete Greig, *Dirty Glory: Go Where Your Best Prayers Take You* (Red Moon Chronicles Book 2) (Colorado Springs: The Navigators, 2016), 38, Kindle.

2. A. W. Tozer, *That Incredible Christian* (Chicago: Moody, 1964), 46.

3. "The Minor Works of Saint John of the Cross," Catholic Spiritual Direction, accessed March 8, 2021, https://www.jesus-passion.com/Minor_Works_StJohn.htm.

4. Tozer, *That Incredible Christian*, 46.

Chapter 11: The Immense Value of Human Life

1. C. S. Lewis, *The Weight of Glory* (San Francisco: HarperOne, 2001), 45-46.

2. Name changed to protect Thaddeus' human dignity.

3. John F. Kilner, *Dignity and Destiny* (Grand Rapids, MI: Wm. B. Eerdmans Publishing Co., 2015), Intro., Kindle.

4. Matthew 6:26, possibly Matthew 8:28-32, Matthew 10:29-31

5. Sire, *The Universe Next Door*, 34-35.

6. Wesley J. Smith, *A Rat Is a Pig Is a Dog Is a Boy: The Human Cost of the Animal Rights Movement* (New York: Encounter Books, 2012), 363-364, Kindle.

7. Johnson, Alan R., "Context-Sensitive Evangelism in the Thai Setting: Building Capacity to Share Good News," in *Becoming the People of God*, Seanet Series, ed. Paul DeNeui (Pasadena, CA: William Carey Library, 2015), 63-92.

8. Barbara Johnson, *God's Most Precious Jewels are Crystallized Tears* (Nashville: W. Publishing Group, 2001), 132.

Chapter 12: How We See People Impacts How We Treat Them

1.   Viktor E. Frankl, *The Doctor and the Soul* (New York: Vintage Books), Intro., Kindle.

2.   John F. Crosby, "The Witness of Dietrich von Hildebrand," First Things, accessed October 26, 2020, https://www.firstthings.com/article/2006/12/the-witness-of-dietrich-von-hildebrand.

3.   Gary B. Ferngren, "A New Era in Roman Healthcare," Christian History Institute, accessed September 16, 2020, https://christianhistoryinstitute.org/magazine/article/new-era-in-roman-healthcare.

4.   Kilner, *Dignity and Destiny*, 8-10.

5.   Glen Scrivener, "Responding to Pandemics: 4 Lessons from Church History," March 16, 2020, The Gospel Coalition, accessed June 8, 2020, https://www.thegospelcoalition.org/article/4-lessons-church-history/.

6.   Paul Copan, *Is God a Moral Monster?* (Grand Rapids, MI: Baker Publishing Group, 2001), 218, Kindle.

7.   Theodoret of Cyrus (Cyrrhus in Syria), *The Ecclesiastical History*, Book V, Chapter XXVI: Of Honorius the Emperor and Telemachus the Monk.

8.   Rodney Stark, *For the Glory of God* (Princeton: Princeton University Press), 291, Kindle.

9.   Ibid.

10. Daniel F. Stramara Jr., "Gregory of Nyssa: An Ardent Abolitionist," *St. Vladimir's Theological Quarterly* 41, no. 1 (1997): 38-50.

11. David Kelly, "Saint Patrick's Confessio," Patricus, accessed September 28, 2020, https://www.confessio.ie/more/article_kelly#.

12. Stark, *For the Glory of God*, 329.

13. Ibid., 291, 299.

14. Ibid.

15. Ibid., 343-344.

16. Ibid., 340.

17. Hugh Thomas, *The Slave Trade* (New York: Simon & Schuster, 1997), 471-472.

18. V. Chapman Smith, "American Anti-Slavery and Civil Rights Timeline," US History, accessed November 2, 2020, https://www.ushistory.org/more/timeline.htm.

19. History.com Editors, "Sojourner Truth," History, October 29, 2009 (updated January 16, 2020), accessed May 28, 2020, https://www.history.com/topics/black-history/sojourner-truth.

20. Stark, *For the Glory of God*, 349.

21. David Livingstone, *Expedition to the Zambesi* (London: Gerald Duckworth & Co. Ltd, 2001), 293.

22. Pete Greig, *Dirty Glory: Go Where Your Best Prayers Take You*, Red Moon Chronicles Book 2 (Colorado Springs: The Navigators, 2016), 242-243, Kindle. See also John Wesley, "Wesley to Wilberforce," Christian History Institute, accessed September 17, 2020, https://christianhistory institute.org/magazine/article/wesley-to-wilberforce.

23. British forces achieved their goal far sooner than did abolition forces in America. The British slave-owners lived in distant colonies, so their political influence was limited. Second, the British government was far less representative and more centralized than America's government. Britain also borrowed an immense amount of money and paid slave owners

compensation for releasing their slaves. This debt was not repaid until 2015.

24. Kilner, *Dignity and Destiny*, 8-10.

25. Rodney Stark, *The Rise of Christianity* (San Francisco: Harper, 1996), 104-105.

26. John Ortberg, *Love Beyond Reason* (Grand Rapids, MI: Zondervan, 1998), 36.

27. Keller, *The Reason for God*, 66-67.

28. Ibid.

Chapter 14: Seeing Our Own Worth

1. LAT Archives, "Among Jordan's Great Games, This Was It," LA Times, accessed June 3, 2021, https://www.latimes.com/archives/la-xpm-1990-03-29-sp-582-story.html

2. "The Bad Breath of Pride," February 5, 2017, Marckinna, accessed October 23, 2020, https://marckinna.wordpress.com/2017/02/05/the-bad-breath-of-pride/.

3. "Do You Know Who I Am?" Best Clean Funny Jokes. March 26, 2016. https://bestcleanfunnyjokes.com/do-you-know-who-i-am/.

4. Richard Rohr, *Everything Belongs* (New York: Crossroad, 1999), 103; quoted in Brennan Manning, *Ruthless Trust* (New York: HarperCollins, 2002), 124-126.

5. Greg Laurie, and David Kopp, *The Upside-Down Church* (Wheaton, IL: Tyndale House, 1999), 127.

6. Yiddish Proverb, "Too Humble is Half Proud," Dictionary – Quotes, accessed June 3, 2021,.

7. Manning, *Ruthless Trust*, 120-122.

8. Jonathan Sacks, "From Slavery to Freedom: The Meaning of Passover," April 2, 2015, ABC Religion & Ethics, accessed October 23, 2020, https://www.abc.net.au/religion/from-slavery-to-freedom-the-meaning-of-passover/10098436#:~:text=It%20took%20a%20new%20generation,Egypt%20out%20of%20the%20Israelites.%22.

9. Helmut Thielicke, *Nihilism*, trans. John W. Doberstein (London: Routledge and Kegan Paul, 1962), 110, quoted in Sire, *Universe Next Door*, 35.

10. Mark Batterson, *Whisper* (Colorado Spring: The Crown Publishing Group, 2017), chap. 2, Kindle.

11. Thielicke, *Nihilism*, 35.

Chapter 15: Refusing Lies

1. The first five of these lies are commonly attributed to Henry Nouwen.

Chapter 16: Jesus' Last Command: The Great Commission

1. "Missionary Bio's: Hudson Taylor," MB Missions Box, accessed May 30, 2021, https://missionsbox.org/missionary-bio/hudson-taylor/.

2. "Bringing Definition to the Unfinished Task," Joshua Project, May 30, 2021, https://joshuaproject.net.

3. "Status of Global Christianity, 2020, in the Context of 1900-2050," Gordon Conwell, accessed December 11, 2020, https://www.gordonconwell.edu/center-for-global-christianity/wp-content/uploads/sites/13/2020/02/Status-of-Global-Christianity-2020.pdf.

4. J. D. Payne, "Pressure Point #1: Unreached People Groups," JDPayne.org, accessed May 11, 2021, https://www.jdpayne.org/2013/05/pressure-point-1-unreached-peoples/.

5. "Mission Stats: The Current State of the World," The Traveling Team, accessed December 12, 2020, http://www.thetravelingteam.org/stats.

Chapter 17: Discipleship: The Uniqueness of Matthew's Version

1. Jack Canfield and Mark Hansen, *A 5th Portion of Chicken Soup for the Soul* (Cos Cob, CT: Backlist LLC, 2021), 197.

2. Colin Brown, *The New International Dictionary of New Testament Theology*, (Grand Rapids, MI: Zondervan, 1986) 145-146.

3. Scott Allen, *Why Social Justice is not Biblical Justice* (Grand Rapids, MI: Credo House), 176 . See also Nancy Pearcey, *Total Truth: Liberating Christianity from Its Cultural Captivity* (Wheaton: Crossway, 2008), 58.

4. Loren Cunningham, *Making Jesus Lord* (Seattle: YWAM, 1988), 134.

5. Loren Cunningham, *The Book that Transforms Nations* (Seattle: YWAM Publishing, 2007) 46-47.

6. Ibid., 59.

7. Kuyper's spheres were self-government (the individual accountable to God), family government, church government, civil government, and societal government (voluntary associations such as clubs, businesses, and organizations). Cunningham, *The Book that Transforms Nations*, 59.

8. Nancy Pearcey, *Total Truth* (Wheaton: Crossway, 2004), 50.

Chapter 18: Proclamation: The Uniqueness of Mark's Version

1. Dick Brogden, *This Gospel: A Collection of Missions Sermons* (Springfield, MO: Live Dead Publishing, 2018), 148-149.

2. David Leatherberry, *Pentecostalism and the Future of Missions* (Springfield, MO: Global Initiative, 2013), 20.

3. Brogden, *This Gospel*, 135.

Chapter 19: Power: The Uniqueness of Luke's Version

1. Art Thomas in teaching during the Antioch Conference October 28, 2020.

2. Ibid.

Strategy #1: Go to God in Prayer

1. Abraham Lincoln, "I Have Been Driven…," Quotes. net, accessed October 19, 2020, https://www.quotes.net/ quote/2422.

2. Dan McCollam, *Bending Time: Accessing Heavenly Realities for Abundant Living* (N.p.: Sounds of the Nations, 2019), loc. 690, Kindle.

3. Fritz Rienecker, and Cleon Rogers, *Linguistic Key to the New Testament* (Grand Rapids, MI: Zondervan, 1980), 603.

4. James D. Bratt, ed., *Abraham Kuyper: A Centennial Reader* (Grand Rapids, MI: Eerdmans, 1998), 488. Also available at The Gospel Coalition, accessed November 2, 2020, https://www. thegospelcoalition.org/ article/new-from-tgc-every-square-inch/.

5. Benjamin Franklin, "Constitutional Convention Address on Prayer," American Rhetoric Online Speech Bank, addressed June 28, 1787 (Philadelphia, PA), accessed September 17, 2020, https://www.americanrhetoric.com/speeches/benfranklin. htm.

6. John Piper, *Brothers, We Are Not Professionals* (Nashville: Broadman & Holman, 2002), 56.

Strategy #2: Feed Your Faith with God's Word

1. "The Secret of Life is Theological," *The Alliance Tozer Devotional*, The Alliance, accessed October 23, 2020, https:// www.cmalliance.org/devotions/tozer?id=554.

2. Name changed for security purposes.

3. Most of the children in the Christian orphanages/homes we have visited overseas have a living parent or other relative that the child goes to visit over holidays or breaks. Often the primary reasons children are sent to such homes is access to better education and a reduced financial burden on the child's family.

4. "The Threat of Nuclear Terrorism," The Alliance Tozer Devotional, The Alliance, accessed October 23, 2020, https://www.cmalliance.org/devotions/tozer?id=1246.

5. Debbie Macomber, "Feed Your Faith…," Good Reads, accessed October 23, 2020, https://www.goodreads.com/quotes/324736-feed-your-faith-and-your-doubts-will-starve-to-death. Also attributed to Les Brown, "Feed Your Faith…," Quote Tab, accessed October 23, 2020, https://www.quotetab.com/quotes/by-les-brown.

6. "The Magic Pebbles," in *Chicken Soup for the Teacher's Soul*, Chicken Soup for the Soul, accessed October 23, 2020, https://www.chickensoup.com/book-story/38916/the-magic-pebbles.

7. Richard Foster, *The Celebration of Discipline* (San Francisco: Harper and Row, 1988), 63.

8. Ibid., 64-66.

9. Drew Walsh, "Knowledge is Only Rumor Until it Lives in the Bones," April 17, 2029, Bethel, accessed October 23, 2020, https://www.bethel.ch/updates/80. "This is an ancient saying from the Asaro tribe in Papua New Guinea. It is their inter-tribe mantra to not only know truth but also apply it. For they believe that truth not practiced, truth that does not root itself deep within us and therefore change us from the inside out, exemplifying itself in changed behavior and living - that kind of truth lives merely in our heads and hasn't reached the core of our bones."

Strategy #3: Look beyond the Natural, Immediate World

1. The Arbinger Institute, *Leadership and Self-Deception: Getting out of the Box* (Mumbai: Magna Publishing, 2002), 17.

2. Ibid., 17-18.

3. Ibid., 17-20.

4. Dallas Willard, quoted in J. P. Moreland, *Scientism and Secularism* (Wheaton, IL: Crossway, 2018), 109, Kindle.

5. *Gladiator*, directed by Ridley Scott (2000; Paramount Pictures). This line is spoken by Russell Crowe playing Maximus, a super tough and super smart Roman general.

Strategy #4: Overcome Pride

1. Stephen McCranie, "The Master Has Failed…" Good Reads, accessed October 17, 2020, https://www.goodreads.com/quotes/1252243-the-master-has-failed-more-times-than-the-beginner-has.

2. R. T. Kendall, *The Anointing: Yesterday, Today and Tomorrow* (Lake Mary, FL: Charisma House, 2003), 2424-2425, Kindle.

3. John Maxwell, *Thinking for a Change: 11 Ways Highly Successful People Approach Life and Work* (New York: Warner Books, 2003), 196.

Strategy #5: Pursue Gratitude

1. Alice Morse Earle, "The Clock is Running," Good Reads, accessed June 6, 2021, https://www.goodreads.com/quotes/539882-the-clock-is-running-make-the-most-of-today-time.

2. Mark Batterson, "Mark Batterson on the Power of Living in Wide-Eyed Wonder," December 5, 2019, Relevant Magazine, accessed October 23, 2020, https://www.relevantmagazine.com/faith/mark-batterson-on-the-power-of-living-in-wide-eyed-wonder/.

3. John Maxwell, "Life—It's Worth Doing," Injoy Life Club, March 1999, (Monthly tape mentoring club).

4. Alphonse Karr, "Some People Are Always Grumbling...," Brainy Quote, accessed May 18, 2020, https://i.brainyquote.com/quotes/alphonse_karr_104193?src=p.

5. Lawrence Elliot, George Washington Carver: the Man Who Overcame, (Englewood Cliffs: Prentice Hall, 1966), 155-156.

6. John Perry, *Unshakable Faith* (Sister, OR: Multnomah, 1999), 337-338, 349.

7. Ibid., 344.

8. "Albert Einstein: What He Did and Didn't Say," November 10, 2015, Exploring Your Mind, accessed October 23, 2020, https://exploringyourmind.com/albert-einstein-didnt-say/.

9. Jeff Schreve, "But I Didn't Get as Much!" From His Heart, May 12, accessed November 23, 2020, https://www.crosswalk.com/devotionals/fromhisheart/from-his-heart-week-of-may-25-11542326.html. This story may be apocryphal.

Strategy #6: Gain Perspective from Christ's Body

1. John Maxwell, *The Success Journey* (Nashville: Thomas Nelson, 1997), 62.

2. Jean Johnson, *We Are Not the Hero* (Sisters: Deep River Books, 2012), 5791-5796, Kindle.

3. Kevin Williams (compiler), "Jokes about the Afterlife," Near-death.com, accessed October 23, 2020.

Strategy #7: Seek the Baptism of the Holy Spirit

1. Quoted in John Maxwell, *The 21 Most Powerful Minutes in a Leader's Day* (Nashville: Thomas Nelson, 2000), 27.

2. Denzil R. Miller, *Missionary Tongues Revisited* (Springfield, MO: PneumaLife Publications, 2014), 69.

3. Denzil Miller, *In Step with the Spirit* (Springfield: AIA Publications, 2008), 109-110.

4. Gordon Anderson, "Baptism in the Holy Spirit, Initial Evidence, and a New Model," *Enrichment* (Winter 2005): 76. Denzil Miller, *Empowered* (N.p.: Life Publishers, 2005), 297-298.

5. Denzil Miller, *Empowered* (N.p.: Life Publishers, 2005), 297-298.

Strategy #8: Desire Spiritual Gifts

1. Name changed for security. Abdi is a Muslim who gave his life to Christ.

2. The Antioch Initiative (www.theantiochinitiative.com) is a partnership between Assemblies of God World Missions and North Central University in Minneapolis, MN, focused on the unreached of the world.

3. David Lim, *Spiritual Gifts: A Fresh Look* (Springfield, MO: GPH, 2003), 71-72.

4. Paul York, phone conversation with author, December 11, 2020.

5. Denzil Miller, *Missionary Tongues Revisited: More Than an Evidence* (Springfield, MO: Pneuma life Publications, 2014), 61.

6. Kris Vallotton, *Basic Training for the Prophetic Ministry*, exp. ed. (Shippensburg: Destiny Image, Inc., 2014), 45, Kindle.

7. R. T. Kendall, *The Anointing: Yesterday, Today and Tomorrow* (Lake Mary, FL: Charisma House, 2003), 1757-1760, Kindle.

8. Ibid., 2454-2455, Kindle.

Strategy #9: Keep a Sabbath

1. Ronald Heifetz and Marty Linsky, *Leadership on the Line* (Boston: Harvard Business School Press, 2002), 51.

2. Shuki Friedman, "An Israeli Shabbat," The Israel Democracy Institute, June 23, 2016, accessed September 17, 2020, https://en.idi.org.il/articles/2348#:~:text=The%20Ahad%20Ha'am%20once,keep%20and%20maintain%20the%20Shabbat.

3. John Ortberg, *God is Closer than You Think* (Grand Rapids, MI: Zondervan, 2005), 72. Quoting Abraham Heschel *The Sabbath: Its Meaning for Modern Man*. Boston: Shambhala, 2003, 14.

4. A. J. Swoboda, *Subversive Sabbath: The Surprising Power of Rest in a Nonstop World* (Grand Rapids, MI: Baker Publishing Group, 2018), 67, Kindle.

5. Ibid., 57.

6. Vince Lombardi, "Fatigue…" Brainy Quotes, accessed October 17, 2020, https://www.brainyquote.com/quotes/vince_lombardi_380768.

Strategy #10: Avoid Sin

1. Myra Shelley, Harold Shelley, and Marshall Shelley, The Leadership Secrets of Billy Graham (Grand Rapids, MI: Zondervan, 2005), 65.

2. Charles Swindoll, *Come before Winter and Share My Hope* (Willowdale, ON: R. G. Mitchell Books, 1988), 177-178.

Strategy #11: Eliminate Distortion

1. J. Gresham Machen, "Christianity and Culture," Princeton Theological Review 11 (1913): 7. New Hope Fairfax, accessed June 5, 2021, http://www.newhopefairfax.org/files/Machen.Christianity%20And%20Culture.pdf. Quoted by William Lane Craig, *Reasonable Faith*, 3rd ed. (Wheaton, IL: Crossway Books, 2008), 4, Kindle.

2. "Ponderings with Doug," Natchitoches Parish Journal, January 27, 2017, accessed October 26, 2020, https://natchitochesparishjournal.com/2017/01/27/ponderings-with-doug-january-27-2017/.

3. Steve Backlund, *Let's Just Laugh about That* (N.p.: Steve Backlund, 2011), 7.

4. Martin Luther, "Everything That is Done…," Forbes Quotes, accessed October 20, 2020, https://www.forbes.com/quotes/6679/.

5. Charles Swindoll, *The Tale of the Tardy Oxcart* (Nashville: Word Publishing, 1998), 274.

6. Francis Frangipane, *The Three Battlegrounds* (Cedar Rapids, IA: Arrow Publications, 1989), chap. 5, 308-309, Kindle.

Strategy #12: Obey What God Has Already Revealed

1. Thomas Carlyle, "Go As Far…," Brainy Quote, accessed October 17, 2020, https://www.brainyquote.com/quotes/thomas_carlyle_384486.

2. Eric Liddell, "The Disciplines Of The Christian Life," AZ Quotes, accessed May 26, 2021, .

Strategy #13: Renew and Expand Your Thinking

1. Ralph Waldo Emerson, "People Only See…," Brainy Quotes, accessed October 23, 2020, https://www.brainyquote.com/quotes/ralph_waldo_emerson_101263.

Strategy #14: Focus on God's Greatness

1. A. W. Tozer, *The Knowledge of the Holy* (AW Tozer Series) (Daryaganj, New Delhi: General Press, 2019), 130, Kindle.

Strategy #15: Don't Let Uncertainty Cripple You

1. Corrie ten Boom, *Tramp for the Lord* (Old Tappan: Fleming H. Revell Company, 1974), 12.

2. Ibid.

3. Don Meyer, *Think About It* XII (Phoenixville, PA: University of Valley Forge, 2016), 70-71.

4. Martin Luther King, Jr. "Faith is Taking the First Step…," Brainy Quotes, accessed October 17, 2020, https://www.brainyquote.com/quotes/martin_luther_king_jr_105087.

5. Sinach, "Waymaker," produced by Mayo Muziq, April 7, 2016, YouTube, accessed October 23, 2020, https://www.youtube.com/watch?v=QM8jQHE5AAk.

6. "Worry Hinders Our Faith," Preaching Today, accessed June 2, 2020, https://www.preachingtoday.com/illustrations/2000/november/12718.html.

7. Paul Fritz, "The African Impala Can Jump to a Height of Over 10 Feet," Sermon Central, October 18, 2000, Sermon Central, accessed June 2, 2020, https://www.sermoncentral.com/sermon-illustrations/10933/the-african-impala-can-jump-to-a-height-of-over-by-paul-fritz.

8. Dan Quarrell, "How Fast Does Usain Bolt Run in MPH/KM Per Hour? Is He the Fasted Recorded Human Ever? 100M Record?" Eurosport, December 20, 2016, accessed June 17, 2020, https://www.eurosport.com/athletics/how-fast-does-usain-bolt-run-in-mph-km-per-hour-is-he-the-fastest-recorded-human-ever-100m-record_sto5988142/story.shtml.

9. Mark Batterson, sermon, North Central University chapel, Minneapolis, MN, November 10, 2015.

10. Manning, *Ruthless Trust*, 5.